BOATING FOR BEGINNERS

Jeanette Winterson was born in Lancashire in
1959. After a long tussel she opted out of being a
Charismatic Evangelist, went to Oxford to get
some peace and quiet, and now lives and works
in London. Her first novel, *Oranges Are Not The
Only Fruit*, was published in 1985 and her third
novel, *The Passion*, in 1987.

Also by Jeanette Winterson

Oranges Are Not The Only Fruit
The Passion

Boating for Beginners
JEANETTE WINTERSON

Illustrated by Paula Youens

A Methuen Paperback

BOATING FOR BEGINNERS

First published in Great Britain 1985
and reprinted 1988
by Methuen London Ltd
11 New Fetter Lane, London EC4P 4EE
Copyright © 1985 Jeanette Winterson

Reproduced, printed and bound in Great Britain by
Hazell Watson & Viney Limited,
Member of the BPCC Group,
Alyesbury, Bucks

British Library Cataloguing in Publication Data

Winterson, Jeanette
  Boating for beginners.
  I. Title
  823'.914[F]   PR6073.I55/

ISBN 0-413-59020-8 Pbk

For Philippa Brewster
and Ezra the White Rabbit

Bags of rocks and chunks of Ararat, Turkey,
that Biblical archaeologists believe
are relics of Noah's Ark have been taken
to the US for laboratory analysis.

The Guardian: 28.8.84

At eighteen she realised that she would never have the bone structure to be decadent. . . .

Years of grimacing in the mirror and covering her face in a solution of bone meal had all been wasted. Her nose was snub, her jaw undistinguished, and she was short.

'It's your own fault, Gloria,' scolded her mother. 'You wouldn't take milk as a child.'

She had dreamed of martyrdom, her elegant profile jutting through the flames; she had dreamed of stardom, eager thousands trying to make their cheekbones just like hers. At the very least she might have been a recluse, casting aquiline shadows across her unswept floor. Now, all these things were closed to her, and what was left? She was moderately intelligent, but not very, she had a way with animals, and she wanted to fall in love. She sat down and accepted her fate. Either she could be a secretary or she could be a prostitute. If she chose the latter there would be the problem of what to wear for work and how to arrange her hair (her recent experiments with ash-blond tint had left her threadbare – she should probably have mixed the powder with water instead of bleach).

'I can wear a headscarf if I'm a secretary,' she told herself. Then, a little sadly, 'There's no such thing as a bald prostitute.'

She knew she would have to settle for less money, but she solaced that blow with thoughts of luncheon vouchers and regular hours. One of her mother's magazines was lying on the floor, and although she knew it would end in tears, Gloria picked it up and turned the pages. It was full of people whose jaws could have been used as scythes. They led rich fulfilling lives doing nothing at all and earning vast sums of money. They offered her their beauty tips, cut-price bath oil, and exclusive revealing interviews about their glittering lives. Quickly, Gloria turned to the problem page: acne, period pains, unwanted body hair, fat husbands, ugly wives. She felt a wave of relief. At least some people were still vile, obscure and blotchy. Not for them glamorous bed-hopping and expensive narcotics. Her mother called it sordid, but she still bought the magazines.

'For the recipes,' she said, whenever she caught Gloria's reproachful eye. Certainly the recipes were magnificent: sorbets smothered in cream, passion fruit dripping with Kirsch, breasts of melon spread with honey. Gloria dreamed the tastes while Mrs Munde carried on steaming fish. Her mother was nothing if not regular.

'Brain food,' she declared, and at other times: 'Fish, the Lord's first born.'

Mother and daughter laboured under a highly complex and entirely different understanding of the nature of their relationship. Often, Gloria would look at her mother and wonder who she was. She had been known to pass her in the street and not recognise her. Mrs Munde, on the other hand, fondly believed they shared a common ground other than the one they were sitting on. That night, as dusk fell, and her mother served up the fish, Gloria felt emotional enough to attempt a conversation. Usually she let her mother talk.

'Mother, have you ever been in love?'

'Of course I have: I was in love with your father. He had legs so fine it was a sin to walk on them. The first time I saw him I was lying face-down in the soil crying my eyes out because I'd lost my grass snake. I looked up and there were his legs going up like columns, and oh, at the very top, his head. I thought I was seeing a vision. He spent all day with me trying to find that snake, and at 11 about half past three, I knew I had fallen in love.'

'Did he love you too?'

'No, I don't think he loved me until I made him my chocolate mousse.'

Gloria nodded slowly, stirring the fish pan with a bit of twig. If it could happen to her mother, surely it could happen to her? Perhaps she would marry her boss? Perhaps he would come in one day, and whisk the scarf from her head (her hair was bound to grow again), then murmur something about her being irresistible. She'd let him take her, right there, in front of the water dispenser and afterwards it would be a large house, babies, and endless barbecues on the lawn.

'Mother, I want to be a secretary,' she announced, suddenly and firmly. Her mother sat up from where she had been drawing dust pictures of her first husband (one of the reasons she enjoyed eating outside was the freedom it gave her to do other things).

'You can't be, it's dangerous, I won't let you, you don't know any shorthand, you'll have to drink instant coffee.'

'No I won't,' said Gloria as reasonably as she knew how. 'I'll take the grinder, and I can learn shorthand at school. I want to live in the city and meet interesting men.'

'Whore!' screamed her mother. 'Why don't you just become a prostitute?'

Gloria didn't want to go through all that again, so she just said, 'I'll come home and visit you, I promise.'

Mrs Munde was beside herself. 'I'm not letting you go and live in the city. It's full of gaming clubs and unmentionable practices; you'll get a disease.'

'I'll be careful. I'll share a flat with another girl.'

The mother burst into floods of tears and started to bang her head against the fish kettle. 'If only your father was alive,' she moaned. 'That I should be left to see my only daughter come to this.'

At that moment a low bellow upstaged the mother's din. Gloria got up.

'I've got to go and give Trebor his supper. It's not fair to keep him waiting.' She hurried over to the outhouse where her elephant was gently swinging his trunk. While she got his food ready Gloria talked over her plans, reassuring Trebor: 'Don't worry, I'll take you with me when I go. We'll find a landlady who doesn't mind pets.' The elephant grunted and together they sank into a daydream of what life would be like in the city. . . .

All this was happening a long time ago, before the flood. The Big Flood starring God and Noah and a cast of thousands who never survived to collect their royalty cheques. Of course you know the story because you've read it in the Bible and other popular textbooks, but there's so much more between the lines. It's a block-buster full of infamy, perfidy and frozen food and in just a few hours when you've read this book your life will seem rich and full. . . .

Noah was an ordinary man, bored and fat, running a thriving little pleasure boat company called Boating for Beginners. Gaudily painted cabin cruisers took droves of babbling tourists up and down the Tigris and Euphrates, sightseeing. It was a modest but sound operation. Noah worked hard and was not pleased to see the fruits of his labour slipping away into dubious community projects. That was the trouble with Nineveh: it had become a Socialist state full of immigrants, steel bands and Black Forest Gâteau. He didn't mind a piece of cake himself but a woman's place was in the kitchen. He believed that refrigerators had started the long slide into decadence. Work, good labour-intensive work, was what kept a

society together; and now with all these convenience foods and ready-mixed cocktails there was too much time for agitation and revolution.

Today had been especially depressing. He had opened his morning paper to find that the corrupt Nineveh council had approved yet more taxpayers' money to be spent on providing roller skates for outlying villages without proper public transport. He reached for his heart pills; it was really getting a bit much. Suddenly a huge hand poked out of the sky, holding a leaflet. Trembling, Noah took it. It was yellow with black letters and it said, 'I AM THAT I AM, YAHWEH THE UNPRONOUNCEABLE.'

That's what Noah reported at the press conference he held in the lounge bar of his most luxurious cruiser, *Nightqueen*. He had been chosen, it seemed, to lead the world into a time of peace and prosperity under the guidance of the One True God. Naturally people were curious to know why the Unpronounceable hadn't exposed himself sooner, but Noah told them that only when the time is ripe can miracles happen. The Lord had been graciously biding his time, hoping that mere mortals might sort themselves out, and of course they couldn't: it was still false gods and socialism. Noah admitted that the

Unpronounceable had some explaining to do, but they were collaborating on a manuscript that would be a kind of global history from the beginnings of time showing how the Lord had always been there, always would be there and what a good thing this was. They were anxious to make the book dignified but popular, and had decided to issue it by instalments starting with *Genesis*, or *How I Did It*.

There were sceptics of course, who claimed that Noah had made up the whole story to get more publicity for his company. Noah had anticipated such ungracious behaviour from the media, and so at midnight, on the eve of another press conference, he asked everyone to come out on deck and look up. While they were looking up, Noah fell down on his knees and begged his God to have mercy on these sinners, forgive their hard and doubting hearts and show himself in all his glory. There was a distant rumble, the river lit up with a strange luminescence and from out of the sky came a large vibrating cloud. By this time all the hard and doubting hearts had spilt their wine and Noah was shouting: 'Glory, Lord, Glory!' For a few moments the cloud hovered, then veered away in dazzling loops, leaving a message in the night for all to see: GOD IS LOVE, DON'T MESS WITH ME.

'A miracle, a miracle!' screamed Noah. 'Put your donations in the box.'

The next morning Noah began to delegate. He was no longer to be seen checking tarpaulins on the quay, he hired minions for his business, minions for his press releases and an orchestra to take on tour with his forthcoming Glory Crusade. He believed that the personal is political, bought up a national newspaper and began to attack the Nineveh Council for what he called 'wanton and ungodly spending'. To a seeming majority his beliefs and vigorous social attitudes were a welcome relief. There was no need, after all, to be vegetarian, charitable and feminist. Noah promised a return to real values and, if possible, the Gold Standard; and he had the backing of the Unpronounceable who couldn't be wrong because he was God. When the Glory Crusade got under way, Noah found himself leading thousands of people to the knees of the Lord. No one could resist a world where men and women knew exactly what they were doing and who they were doing it for; it made life simple and sunny again.

Of course, there were sacrifices that had to be made, like convenience foods and refrigerators. 'A simple diet,' said Noah, 'is more important than gold.' (He meant this as a metaphor only.) 'A simple diet prepared by a simple wife, these are the corner-stones of a godly life.' Later this became a postcard and a huge success – so much so that Noah followed it up with another postcard showing a plate of green vegetables. Around the border it said, 'In the Eternal City there will be no refrigerators.'

The Glory Crusade toured all the major spots around Ur of the Chaldees, and one night Mrs Munde was drawn inside. She was very impressed – all that white canvas and nice music and young men with regular teeth. She was married, pregnant and bewildered, and when Noah asked if anyone truly wanted to be happy, she put up her hand and lost her heart.

When her daughter was born, her husband had wanted to call the child Veronica after his favourite film star, but the mother knew better than that. The child would be called Gloria after the Glory Crusade, and it was Mrs Munde's one hope that her daughter should serve the Unpronounceable in some spectacular way.

When Gloria was five, Noah had announced his retirement from public affairs. He would still make the occasional guest appearance and the crusades would continue without him, but he felt he needed time to himself with the Lord to get on with their book. *Genesis* or *How I Did It* had sold out over and over again, as had the second volume *Exodus* or *Your Way Lies There*. Noah felt that he and the Lord should concentrate on something a bit more philosophical about the role of priests and things; and then there was the Good Food Guide they were planning: what to eat on a long haul across the desert etc. So with reluctance he was going to be a recluse. As he made this announcement, he also advertised for a personal cook of the very highest standard – which meant cooking over an open fire with the most primitive equipment. Mrs Munde applied because she'd done just that all her life. She got the job.

Thirteen years passed, Mr Munde died of neglect and Gloria grew up thoughtful and a little unbalanced. She was a passionate child and it did her no good at all to read her mother's endless collection of romantic fiction written by Bunny Mix, the most famous romantic novelist of them all. Noah particularly enjoyed having celebrities espouse his cause, and one of the most vocal was Bunny Mix, who believed in the purity of love between men and women, the importance of courtship and the absolute taboo of sex before marriage. She had written almost one thousand novels, all of which had the same plot, but she was clever enough to rotate the colour of the heroine's hair and the hero's occupation so that you never felt you were actually reading the same book twice in a row. Sometimes they were even set in different places. Not only had Bunny made a fortune out of novels; she was also the author of a cookery book and a volume of love letters written by rapists, despots and adulterers to their mistresses. She overlooked this contradiction, urging her readers to wallow in the beauty of the prose, which despite all the sinfulness behind it was certainly much better than her own.

It was perhaps this book alone that had saved Gloria from becoming a complete emotional invertebrate. She could quote all of the letters by heart and often did in times of great stress, such times usually being the hours spent in the company of her mother. Because Bunny Mix was such a good friend of Noah's and she often dedicated her books to him as the regenerator (along with herself) of tattered morality, Noah had a whole collection which he generously passed on to Mrs Munde. The mother loved to read them after work, and sometimes she and Gloria would sit by the firelight taking a chapter each and reading aloud.

Mrs Munde had never thought that Gloria would want to leave their little home, especially after she had scrimped and saved to give her trombone lessons so that she could join the Good News Orchestra. The idea of her daughter going to live in the city, never eating properly and most likely meeting an unsuitable man filled her with horror. She had to act quickly, and the only thing she could think of was to speak to Noah as soon as Gloria had settled the elephant and gone to sleep. Noah never slept, so Mrs Munde didn't worry about the time.

When the world was quiet, she put on her hat and coat and set off up the hill to the big house. It was guarded, but after all these years she had no problems getting in. Whether it was her fish or chocolate mousse, Mrs Munde had a place in Noah's affections – not a very large place, more of a studio flat, but he liked to protect his workers and why not give Gloria a job? She could help him with his latest, most sensational and most secret project.

When Mrs Munde came outside again she felt like a young faun in spring. Her worries were over. True, it was not quite what she had had in mind for her child, but as long as Gloria kept up with her trombone and in with Noah she would no doubt be able to improve herself later. Her euphoria was such that even the sight of the elephant gently eating her black-out curtain was too insignificant to give her a headache. She pushed him out of the parlour, lay down on her mat and fell asleep. . . .

Next morning Gloria woke early. She liked the mornings, when she could pretend she was the only person on earth apart from a mysterious stranger who left her love notes under convenient stones. She walked for an hour or so, then wandered back to the shack hoping that her mother might be feeling more flexible. Mrs Munde was sitting on the front step making coffee and looking determined. Gloria's heart began to sink.

'Your elephant ate my black-out curtain again last night. I'm going to have it put down.'

'You can't. I love him. He's mine.'

'He's not house-trained, he's too big . . . but I'll give you one last chance.' (Gloria noticed her mother had an unusual gleam in her eye.) 'Noah's offered you a nice job working with animals. If you decide to take it you can take the elephant too, he can live in. If not, well,' and Mrs Munde made a sinister slitting noise through her teeth. Gloria felt faint and held onto the barbecue set for support.

'I'm not going to live with that transvestite.'

Mrs Munde thought the world had come to an end. 'What did you call him?'

Gloria mustered all her hormones and started again. 'I said he's a transvestite. Look at his clothes. They're not robes, they're frocks, and he wears stacked heels and make-up.'

'That's just for the newspapers,' snapped Mrs Munde. 'They like him to look tall and healthy. He's a star.'

Gloria fell silent. She didn't know or care what Noah was. She'd read about his habits and preferences – inventing strange machines in the middle of the night – in a magazine someone had brought to school, the sort of magazine her mother never allowed in the house. At the time she had been embarrassed because everyone knew her mother was his cook and they all asked her if the report was true. It was the first time that Gloria had been shocked out of her autonomous inner life. She lived at the bottom of a deep pool where her mother and the rest of the world were only seen as vague shadows on the surface. Now she was being forced into a graceless breaststroke to find out what everyone else was talking about.

'I'll leave you to think about it.' Her mother bustled
away.

In despair Gloria did a personality test in one of the
glossies. She didn't have the drive to be a banker, she
didn't have the body to be a croupier and she already
knew she didn't have enough hair to be a prostitute. It
seemed like she and Trebor would be going to stay with
Noah after all. She wasn't religious, because she had
always associated that state with fish which she didn't
like eating and a musical instrument she hated playing.
Still, from what she'd heard Noah wasn't very religious
either, and there was always the possibility that she might
meet Bunny Mix and get a signed copy. In her own way
Gloria was adaptable, and so she began to deflate the
balloon that held her vision of the city and puffed away
instead on a new one marked 'Noah'.

Like Gloria, Mrs Munde was by nature philosophical
and optimistic. She believed in the power of the mind –
at least, those minds in harmony with the will of the
Unpronounceable. After her meeting with Noah she felt
more fulfilled as a mother; she felt she had come closer to
grasping that elusive and mythic image most perfectly
described in Bunny Mix's novels. Every young girl needed
a good mother, a figure who could be both wise and
sympathetic, a model for the future and a comfort for the
present. Her own mother had been little more than a
useless socialite, whose dedication to pleasure had seemed
shocking to the impressionable and earnest girl who
became Mrs Munde – earnest, because she had wanted
more than anything to be an astronomer; indeed she had
spent nearly all her youth gazing out of the window,
wondering about the nature of the cosmos and how she
could truly be part of it. As she grew older and her
ambitions remained as distant as their object, she persuaded herself that this early impulse was really a metaphor for something else, and when she heard about the
Unpronounceable she knew her instinct had been correct.

She was an Astronomer without Telescope. Now the cosmos loomed larger and more definable, and she belonged to it. She had been fixed on the creation when what she was seeking was the creator. Suddenly, her life collapsed into place.

Gloria was more of a problem. As far as Mrs Munde could see, her daughter had no ambition and no faith. It never occurred to her that Gloria had chosen to be nothing in order to avoid being her mother's something. Only by remaining in a vacuum-sealed diving bell could Gloria hope to avoid the storm at sea that was Mrs Munde. And so, Gloria's vision of life was rather like the Lady of Shalott's. She dared not expose herself to the genuine and unruly three-dimensional world that included her mother. If she did that, she had a feeling something awful would become inevitable. Instead, she peered through her misty porthole on the shadowy world and dreamed of being rescued by somebody tall. . . .

What Mrs Munde hadn't yet told Gloria about her new job was the possibility it brought of fame. She wasn't going to clean out the chickens or work with dogs; she was going to be part of a special team who were collecting animals for Noah's latest dazzling venture: a touring stage epic about the world and how the Unpronounceable had made it.

Stunned by the success of their literary collaboration Noah and God had decided to dramatise the first two books, bringing in Bunny Mix to add legitimate spice and romantic interest. The cast would be large, probably most of Ur of the Chaldees, and the animals would take pride of place. The whole show was to tour the heathen places of the world, like York and Wakefield, in a gigantic ship built especially by Noah's most experienced men. As it happened, a film company would be putting the whole thing on camera, not just the play itself but the making of the play, because Noah claimed he was going to carry his ship over a mountain by a miracle. This was thought to be nonsense, but it was bound to make money. There was the problem of casting, but it had been decided, quite fairly, that Noah's three sons and their wives should take the major roles. After all they were a public family, unlikely to be upset by the personal intrusions that accompany stardom. Ham and Shem were to play different aspects of YAHWEH because everyone agreed that God is a multifaceted and complex character who shouldn't be restricted by a single actor. Japeth was to play his father. Excitement was mounting amongst the privileged few who knew how Bunny Mix would interpret the characters of the overthrown goddesses collectively described as The Trivia. They had to be seductive but not too racy, and they had to lose all sympathy before the Unpronounceable finally destroyed them. A difficult task, but Bunny was a wonderful woman.

Mrs Munde mused on what she had been told, longing for the morning when the announcement was officially to be made. Perhaps Gloria would get a small part, maybe as one of the more musical heathen. Even if she didn't she'd still have a break in theatre production, and what mother could do more? She had given her only daughter a proper start in life; she had every right to feel proud.

The morning came, and of course the announcement was in all the papers. The *Tablet* had an old photograph of Noah raising someone from the dead, and a long description of the play and forthcoming film. The whole town was gossiping and doing their hair in case a scout came by looking for faces. The greatest excitement was generated by the imminent return of Japeth and Ham and Shem with their lovely wives Sheila, Desi and Rita. Japeth the jewellery king, Ham the owner of that prestigious pastrami store, More Meat, and Shem, once playboy and entrepreneur, now a reformed and zealous pop singer.

Bliss was it in that dawn to be alive, but to be young the very heaven. Ur of the Chaldees looked less and less like an inhabited spittoon and more and more like Milton

Keynes as the hours ticked by. Neighbours made friendly gestures and lent one another their lawn mowers, the dustbin men volunteered to return to work without their extra 10 per cent and the *Socialist Worker Party Magazine* painted their offices. It's extraordinary what Art can do.

Gloria was less certain. She had always considered the theatre a rather *risqué* profession and she said as much to her mother.

'Don't be silly,' cooed Mrs Munde. 'This isn't State-subsidised Nineveh Council theatre, this is honest profit and the glory of the Lord. You won't find any drugs or loose living, and remember it's being made into a film. You should be thankful for your chances and especially grateful to me.'

For a moment Gloria felt her diving bell keel to one side: her mother had managed to score a direct hit despite eighteen years of careful preparation. Was there no justice in the world? No. She thought about an article she had once seen on mind control. Apparently if there was a person fiendish enough to set about interfering with your life, the only thing you could do was to concentrate hard on someone they were unlikely ever to have heard of called Martin Amis. The particular blankness of this image was guaranteed to protect from any subtle force, but Gloria realised with a sinking heart that it was too late now.

Mrs Munde broke into this miasma. 'You have to go up to the big house in the morning and you'll be told how to get started. I won't be here much myself because Noah wants me to try out a few new recipes that need some invention of his. Do you know he's been inventing in his spare time? No, I don't suppose you do, you never listen to what I tell you. Well Noah's not just religious, he's scientific and he's invented all kinds of things, including a jet-propelled shark to amuse the tourists. He's going to do the special effects for the film. You should be proud,

Gloria; I know I am. I look up at the stars, those bright and pleading stars, and I feel proud.' Mrs Munde began to choke and Gloria was forced to approximate intimacy and slap her on the back. She felt about touching her mother the way natives feel about looking into a camera: her soul might be transferred by accident.

'I think I'll go to bed,' she said, 'so that I can do my best in the morning,' and she folded the night around her with something like hope. Surely things couldn't get worse?

'I was like a disaster looking for somewhere to happen,' said Doris, which seemed to Gloria a very intimate and surprising thing for a perfect stranger to say. They were standing in a long room in Noah's house and Doris was doing the dusting. 'I've been hired, same as you, to help with the arrangements, so we're going to see a lot of each other.'

Gloria wasn't sure which question to ask first; she wanted to know about Doris and her disastrous self, but she needed to know what these arrangements were. Not used to making choices, Gloria just frowned. It had started to dawn on her as she surfaced from her pool that she was remarkably under-equipped to deal with life as it is lived. Her own world had been perfectly ordered and very clean because she had assembled it from a kit composed of spiritual certainties and romantic love. It didn't matter that she hardly believed in God and had only ever received one valentine. What did matter was the voltage of faith she injected into every worn-out cliché. A rose is a rose is a rose.

'Yes,' continued Doris, 'all my life I've hovered over happiness like a black cloud. Whatever I've touched has turned to dross.'

('Dross?' wondered Gloria, too nervous to interrupt.)

'I used to be rich and beautiful. I took my holidays in

Andorra, and now I have to use a false name just to get a cleaning job. I don't think it's my fault. We're all drunken mice running round on the wheel of fortune and some of us are lucky and some of us aren't.'

Lucky. This was one word Gloria recognised. She clutched at it.

'Don't you feel lucky then?'

Doris gave a hard and bitter laugh. 'My first husband died on our honeymoon, my second suffocated at a fancy-dress party and my eldest boy is an accountant.'

There was a silence while Gloria hopped from foot to foot, trying to design her first social response. Unaware of this new architecture going on around her Doris felt the silence compelled her to continue.

'I've learned something though. I think of myself as a student of life. I suppose you could call me an organic philosopher.'

'Do you understand the Meaning of Life?' blurted out Gloria. She knew that everyone sought this mysterious meaning because it was in all the magazines. Every month there was an article on how to be fulfilled and what to invest in when you were. Gloria felt tense at the thought of being offered a fully inflated lifebelt to help her nego-tiate the pool.

'The Meaning of Life,' began Doris slowly, 'is death.' Gloria looked blank. 'All your clothes are rotting, all your food is putrefying, you're covered in dead skin and your bowels are full of muck. Why try and pretend? No wonder we don't have an easy life.'

'What about freezer food? That's not rotting.' Gloria hoped her mother couldn't hear.

'I'm not talking about things that have been interfered with. I'm talking about Essences. Decay is the key; once you've come to terms with decay not much can disappoint you. Your house will crumble, your friends will die. Nothing remains. Can you think of anything permanent?' She turned on Gloria with a challenging duster.

'Washing up,' cried Gloria wildly. 'There's always washing up to do. No matter how much you manage, there's always more.'

Doris was thoughtful. 'Washing up as a Metaphor. I can see what you mean.' Gloria had said the right thing. It had never happened to her before and she actually felt rather tearful.

It's fortunate that our dangerously emotional moments are often punctured by Gross Reality (one reason for the Shakespearean fool). The lives of fanatics are usually rather low on Gross Reality, which allows them to take their visions too seriously. Joan of Arc or Mary Baker Eddy might have found their personal lives less complicated if, say, either of them had had a bowel complaint or a passion for chocolate milkshakes. If Gloria had been left untended a moment longer the effect of that first wave of social rapport might have drowned her for good; but by a miracle she survived, and that miracle appeared in the form of Rita, Sheila and Desi, fresh from the hairdresser's.

Rita was dark-skinned with a bush of orange hair and matching painted fingernails. Gloria had never seen anyone wearing a leopard-skin dress in the day before. Even the models in the magazines wore them against a photo-background that was clearly night. Exhausted from her recent efforts Gloria found she could think of nothing to say, so she turned to stare at Sheila who was very fat and covered from head to foot in solid gold. She had a snake torque round her neck, snakes dangling from her ears, snake ankle chains and something like a boa constrictor round her middle. She was the most unsnakelike creature Gloria had ever seen. Beside these two, Desi appeared relatively normal, clad as she was in a designer-cut suede cat suit. Gloria noticed that she wasn't wearing make-up but that her hair was probably henna'ed.

'Hi,' said Sheila. 'Guess you know who we are because we're wearing our badges. You should have a name badge too if you're working here. Are you with the film crew or the stage hands?'

'Neither,' said Doris loudly. 'I'm here to do the cleaning and she's here for . . .' Doris stopped as she realised she had no idea who she'd been talking to, but then, she thought to herself, knowing is a superficial position to assume, most commonly in fact a deception. Comforted by this she went back to her dusting, but Sheila vulgarly pursued the point. 'So tell us, skinny, what do you do here? We don't know anyone. We've just arrived.'

('Americans,' thought Doris. 'Typical.')

Gloria breathed deeply twice and concentrated on Martin Amis in an effort to clear her mind. 'I'm here to help with the animals.'

'Shit,' said Sheila, 'you a zoo keeper?'

'No.' Gloria was getting agitated. 'My mother's a cook and I've got an elephant that needs a home and they told me I could bring him with me if I came to work here. I only started this morning and I'm waiting for someone to tell me what to do next.' Gloria wasn't aware of it, but she had just summed up her whole life in one sentence.

'Well, you won't have much animal work for this week; they're still building the set. Tell you what, you can help the girls and me check out our franchises. We're not just film stars, we've got business on our minds as well, ain't that right?'

'Right,' agreed Rita.

('No sense of proportion,' thought Doris bitterly, as she dusted a map of the world as dictated by the Unpronounceable.)

'What do you do?' asked Gloria timidly.

'One of the things we do is to run a kind of clinic, a place to help people who have problems, personal problems with their bodies and themselves. We used to do it just as a hobby but the thing took off and now it's so popular we have to franchise out. We're taking this opportunity to visit our branches and maybe put in a few guest appearances. You can come along, take notes, make coffee, go out for sandwiches.'

'Like a secretary,' whispered Gloria to herself, feeling better.

'Meet us down town first thing tomorrow, outside the Pizza Hut,' ordered Sheila, and the three of them left.

Doris poked her tufted head round the bust of Noah as a young man. 'What kind of people do they think they are? Coming in here ordering me about. You should have refused. I always do. Whenever I'm asked to step outside my Union-defined bounds I refuse, otherwise it's only a matter of time and we workers will be back on collar and lead.'

'I don't belong to a union,' explained Gloria.

'You what! You don't belong to a union and you don't know anything about the transience of existence! No wonder you haven't got on in the world. You're a fool to yourself.'

But Gloria didn't care. Any port in a storm.

Spiritual empathy, coincidence, or sheer bloody-mindedness meant that Mrs Munde was having a difficult time of it too. She had gone up to the house to make scrambled eggs with wheatgerm and found Noah's eldest son, Ham, wandering around her primitive kitchen. Naturally she felt aggrieved. Some places you share with others and some you don't. A room of her own was important to Mrs Munde. She liked to think or to look at her plan of the constellations when she had a spare moment. Now it was going to be small talk and a smiling face when she could have been studying Orion. She decided to make as much noise and mess as possible in order to drive the stranger away. Accordingly she began to sing the overture from *Carmen* while spilling a pail of milk. Ham didn't seem to notice. He was fiddling with some new kitchen item which Mrs Munde assumed to be the promised gadget invented by Noah. A sense of social hierarchy prevented Mrs Munde from actually telling the lousy bastard to get out, so instead she began to think evil thoughts. She had once read an article on mind control, explaining that the best way to bend someone to your will was to think of a gooey mudlike substance called Cliff Richard and direct it at the object of your intent. Such were the marshmallow-suffocating properties of this image that the victim fell instantly into an undignified froth. Putty in your hands in fact. It didn't seem to work. The stranger was insensitive as well as intrusive. Mrs Munde gave it one last go till the kitchen air was thick with Cliff Richard. The stranger suddenly made a little squeaking noise and fell sideways.

'Stop it, stop it!' he cried. 'You're pulping my brain.'

'Well go away then,' sulked Mrs Munde, releasing her

victim, not through generosity but because she found the image too nauseating to continue.

'But I've got something very exciting to say. This conversation could change your life.'

'I've got all the insurance I need,' said Mrs Munde stiffly.

'Lady, I'm not here to sell you anything. I'm here to give you something.'

Mrs Munde looked up into Ham's dark brown eyes, and with a wave of affection that began in her throat and sank to her apron pocket, she felt she might trust this man. Perhaps he had been sent by the Lord. Perhaps he was an angel in disguise come to test her spirit.

'Why don't I take us both for a cup of coffee?' he suggested.

'It's happening to me!' Mrs Munde thrilled inside. 'I've read about it and now it's happening. Perhaps I've been chosen for the Bunny Mix Romance Show.'

The Bunny Mix Romance Show was a very popular afternoon programme in which a woman would be pleasantly accosted by a mysterious tall figure. If she behaved in a fitting and simpering manner a number of boys would then rush onto the set singing in barbershop harmony and strewing flowers. The lucky woman would then be taken out to dinner and given a signed copy in calfskin of her favourite Bunny novel. If she behaved rudely a bucket of custard was poured over her from behind. It was possible that Mrs Munde had already qualified for the custard, which made her nervous because she was allergic to milk. Still, perhaps she could make up for her recent ill temper; and after all, she had never been taken out for a cup of coffee.

As they set off together Ham explained who he was, and Mrs Munde was caught between a welter of disappointment that she wasn't on the Bunny Mix Show after all, and a deluge of wonder that someone so rich and well connected should want to be with her. She decided to be happy.

Ham ordered a double espresso for him and a cappuccino for her. 'Mrs Munde,' he began earnestly, 'do you honestly care about the Lord?'

'Oh I do, I do. No one more.'

Ham nodded and smiled. 'Do you think you would like to serve more fully in countless little ways?'

'Oh I would, I would. It's my dearest wish.'

'Do you think you could cope with long hours and hardship for his sake?'

'Mr Ham, I could cope with a bed of nails for his sake.' (Like Gloria, Mrs Munde was given to bouts of emotional hyperbole.)

'Our God is not a namby-pamby socialist idol, Mrs Munde. He demands we use our brains, our business brains for greater glory and greater profit. He asks us to be worthy of him, and he has said that whatever we do he will bless.'

'The Lord blesses me,' interjected Mrs Munde fervently.

'You may know that I own a fabulously large, forever-expanding chain of pastrami stores called More Meat. I own those stores for His Sake, not my own. He has guided me through the money markets and the loopholes in the Health and Safety Regulations because he is more than YAHWEH, the God of Love, he is YAHWEH the Omnipotent Stockbroker and YAHWEH the Omniscient Lawyer. (Praise Him.) Now he is guiding me to a new place, a place of peace and prosperity because he saw how I was crying out when my profits fell and I couldn't afford to worship him in the style I had promised. He came to me in a vision as I stood over my bank statement and he said, "HAM, THERE IS NO FIXED MINIMUM WAGE IN THE CATERING INDUSTRY." Those were his very words, and I fell on my knees crying, "Thank you, Lord. I will start up a chain of restaurants in your name and I'm going to call them House of Trust and Fortitude." What do you think, Mrs Munde?'

'I think you have the Lord with you mightily, sir,' sighed Mrs Munde. Ham saw that they were both overcome, so he ordered two more coffees. Gulping down his fresh espresso he fixed his magnetic gaze back on Mrs Munde's shining face.

'I need your help. You can cook over an open flame like no other woman of the Lord I know. My father trusts you. I want you to help me prepare and patent a menu in keeping with our faith – though of course we'll have to buy the materials in bulk which might mean a slight drop in standards, but nothing to worry about, and we'll have to be able to work quickly. That machine in your kitchen. It's a hamburger press and I want it for the staple item on our menu, the Hallelujah Hamburger, served with fries and mixed salad. What do you say?'

What could she say? All her life she'd been hungry for a role. She had felt fulfilled in Noah's kitchen, but to be an Evangelist in the kitchens of the world, that was a calling. She straightened her back and smiled.

'I want to do His Will, and I see that, like your father, you have the Spirit of the Unpronounceable. Whatever I can do for you will be a service and a joy.'

Together they walked back to the kitchen and Ham showed Mrs Munde how to use Noah's invention. It was rather like a cement mixer at one end where the meat had to be funnelled, and at the other end a squat attachment plopped out the hamburger cakes.

'Be careful,' warned Ham, 'the motor's very powerful. Now why don't you see how many you can produce in an hour? I'll come back.'

Left alone, Mrs Munde sat down on her favourite stool and opened her astronomy book for comfort. She was overwhelmed. 'The Unpronounceable has chosen me,' she thought. 'If only he chooses Gloria too.'

Gloria had a restless night. She dreamed she was walking in a forest of sugar cane and whenever she opened her mouth to say something all her teeth fell out. Struggling from this sticky dream she slid over the edge of her hammock and tried to remember the important words she had been unable to speak. She opened and shut her mouth a few times beginning each sentence with 'I', and suddenly, like a medium with a message from the other side, she said, in spite of herself, 'I want to be a success.' No sooner had she spoken these words than a bright orange demon hovered in front of her nose holding a pen and a bit of paper. 'Just sign here,' it told her cheerfully. 'There's more to life than honest toil.'

'What am I doing?' asked Gloria, becoming more her usual self again.

'You're making an investment,' replied the shiny creature. 'I promise you, you won't regret this. Your life is about to change.' Feebly Gloria signed and flopped back into a deep sleep. Did she dream it or did it happen?

While a team of highly trained non-union carpenters sawed and planed at Noah's Ark, Gloria waited outside the Pizza Hut hoping no one would take her for a waitress. The trio of wives appeared in similarly alarming outfits, slapped her on the back and took her round to a side door.

'In our kind of business you can't be too careful. People like to think they come to therapy unobserved, but you'll learn.' Sheila was cheerful.

Inside, Gloria saw a set of rooms tastefully decorated in a very pale green. There was a long green couch and a number of attractive pot plants.

'This is one of our most successful sublets because it's in a rich part of town, and there does seem to be a relationship between wealth and the inner life. If you aren't rich you don't tend to want a shrink. Don't ask me

why not, it's just one of those strange and wonderful little
equations.'

Gloria was thankful that Desi was a little more lucid than her relations. At least she now had some idea of what was going on.

'We handle people who can't come to terms with either their sexuality or their chosen expression of it,' she continued.

Then Rita butted in: 'Yeah, we tell them that *we're all God's children* and they can have a great time just as they are. We don't lay anything heavy on them.'

Gloria wondered how Noah reacted to such an attitude in his daughter-in-law.

'Oh, he knows what we do. It's just a different end of the business. Noah doesn't contradict himself. Like the great Unpronounceable, he contains multitudes.'

Dimly Gloria began to perceive a world of affairs beyond her previous dreams. She realised that there is no such thing as a standard. Oddly enough, her heart gave a little skip.

'I've arranged for you to take Fatima's clients for the day, Desi,' said Rita. 'You know most of them and they'll be pleased to see you. We'll meet you for some food up front at six-ish.'

Desi nodded and suggested that Gloria stay with her. Just after the other two had left, there was a tap at the door and a very attractive woman of about thirty glided inside. She sat down in the chair while Desi lay on the couch; and after a few pleasantries and a brief explanation of why she wasn't seeing Fatima, the woman began her story.

'It's been a dreadful week. I can't tell you how dreadful, but I'm going to have a try. You will know from my case notes that my life is ruined by fantasies, fantasies of a particular nature.' (She lowered her voice.) 'These fantasies are about my piano teacher, a bitter blow because I started to learn the piano as a diversion from my previous set of wicked daydreams which involved the boy at our local garden centre – you know my husband has a prize exhibit.' Desi nodded and looked concerned. The woman's face twisted into an expression of pain. 'I could cope with my little thoughts if they didn't intrude so much on my daily life, but now, every time I hear piano music, I have an orgasm – at least I think that's what I have. The problem is they play piano music all the time in the supermarket I use and I find it very difficult to concentrate on my shopping and Gordon, my husband, is very particular about his food. Only yesterday I went in there to buy for a dinner party and I came home with two hundred sachets of lime jelly. I couldn't help it, I was just throwing things into the trolley. The neighbours will notice soon, and I dread meeting anyone I know in there.' She burst into tears and Desi motioned for Gloria to pass the paper hankies.

'You don't have a problem,' Desi said soothingly. 'You need a set of earplugs for potentially dangerous situations; otherwise you should go out and buy all the piano music you can find and make the most of what is quite an unusual experience.'

The woman looked startled. 'Do you really think I'm normal?'

'I think you're normal and lucky,' said Desi firmly. 'Only 35 per cent of all women experience orgasm regularly and 95 per cent of those are self-induced.'

The woman got up and put on her gloves. 'I'm going to the record shop right now and on the way back I'll get those plugs you mentioned and do the shopping. Gordon won't notice, will he?'

'No,' smiled Desi. 'I shouldn't think Gordon will notice a thing.'

Gloria was bewildered again. She had read about orgasms but she thought they were something you only had with men, and only when you were very much in love. She didn't know that you could have them by

yourself or in the supermarket. Bunny Mix sometimes
spoke of the strange thunderclap on the wedding night,
when the bride more or less melted and her new husband
rolled over in tenderness and triumph – because of course
the girl had never before experienced the feeling of true
love. Her mother had always told her never to touch
herself 'down there' and gestured in the region of her
apron pocket. Gloria knew what she meant, and she
didn't even look at it in the bath in case vulgar curiosity
should spoil her own wedding night.

'Do they all talk about orgasms?' she asked Desi, getting
the word out with difficulty.

'Most of the time, yes. But so do we all, except that we
aren't usually paying for it.'

'I don't.' Gloria was prim.

'That's because you've probably never wanted one.'
Desi was teasing but kind. 'Sex is the only thing in life
worth getting emotional about. It's the only thing in life
you should pursue with all your resources. Work is fine,
friends are valuable, but sex is dynamite. It stops you
going mad.'

Gloria had heard it drove you mad. Bunny Mix called
it a terrifying force and cautioned all her readers not to be
ensnared too soon. She felt that even in marriage it should
be measured out; otherwise, she said, it made you limp
and without ambition if you were male, unnatural if you
were female. Babies, she said, should keep your mind off
it.

Desi smiled. 'I like to break down, to forget myself. I
can only do that when another person is affecting me in a
way I can't resist. It's therapy, if you like; perfect and
total therapy.'

This was all a bit intimate for Gloria who preferred the
passive, unimaginable notion of being thunderclapped. If
Bunny Mix was false, whom was she going to trust? The
roses round her heart shrank a little and she resolved to

read one of her old favourites as soon as she could get home.

As she fed herself this emotional Baby Bio, the door opened and a tall person with broad shoulders and expensive clothes walked into the middle of the room. She took one look at Desi and leapt on her like a labrador. 'Denise, it's you! You've come back to me! I knew you would, oh I knew you would. There is a God after all.'

'Hi Marlene,' grinned Desi, disentangling herself. 'We're all back for the film. You must have heard about it.'

'Of course I have,' said Marlene crossly. 'Some of my pottery will be in it, but I didn't think you'd be visiting the clinic. Good, I can tell you all my troubles — and I've got a lot, darling.' She sat down in an elegant heap, then noticed Gloria. 'Who's this?' she demanded.

'This is Gloria, my assistant. Talk to her while I have a pee.'

'She's so coarse,' grumbled Marlene,' 'but I love her. Now what can I tell you about myself? Well, I make designer pots for the most exclusive shop in Nineveh. It helps me to keep calm because I'm a very nervous person who needs a lot of encouragement, so when people tell me how lovely my pots are I feel I can live another day. I used to be a swimmer, one of those synchronised swimmers, but that had to stop when they found out I was having surgery. I mean they weren't nasty or anything, just said that I couldn't compete as a man if I had breasts. They said they gave me extra buoyancy. Now that I'm all woman I haven't the heart to start again. I like the pots more. What do you do in your spare time?'

Gloria thought she was going to die. How did priests ever cope with confessions? They probably didn't. They probably fainted behind the curtain and never told anybody. The person she was sitting next to had no gender identity and still expected Gloria to be able to talk about her hobbies. There must be limits in the world somewhere, she cried to herself. Why had she become the plaything of anarchic forces? Perhaps it was some evil dream or some unscrupulous mind pushing against her own. She no longer had any faith in Martin Amis. All she could do was wait for Desi to come back from the toilet and rescue her. She did.

'So what's the problem, Marlene? You've had the operation, it went well, and I know my sister's a fine needlewoman.'

'Denise,' began Marlene, 'I want it back.'

There was a moment's silence, during which Gloria underwent several reincarnations and returned to her chair weaker than ever.

'Of course, I don't mean the same one. Any one would do, even a smaller one, just so that I could feel it was there. Oh I know I'm wicked and ungrateful but I can hardly walk without it. I used to call it my sleeping snake and now there's only a nest.'

Desi walked over to the couch and sat beside Marlene. She looked worried. 'Marlene, how do you feel about your breasts?'

'Denise, I love my breasts. I go to sleep holding them. I don't want to lose them. I just want it back as well.'

'All right, but there are a few things you should know. First, it's going to be expensive; second, we probably don't have the right colour, and third, it might not work.'

'Oh, I don't care about that,' breathed Marlene. 'I only want it for decoration, so it might be quite nice to have it in a different shade.'

'Come for a pizza at six and talk to Sheila about it,' arranged Desi. 'We'll do what we can.'

When Marlene had left to visit her dentist, Gloria sat back and sighed. 'Desi, are there really people who . . .'

Desi interrupted her. 'There are always people who . . . whatever you can think of. Whatever combination, innovation or desperation, there are always people who . . .'

'Right,' decided Gloria with a sudden firmness. 'I'll find

out,' and her breaststroke assumed a new and purposeful character that almost resembled direction.

Mrs Munde was having trouble with the Hallelujah Hamburger. Noah's machine was slow, messy and smelly. She could have whipped them up quicker with a pastry mould. Truth to tell she was finding the Lord's work altogether tedious. When Ham came back for the third time, she told him they should scrap the machine.

'We can't,' he explained patiently. 'Machines mean cheaper labour. To do this by hand, even if it is quicker, will cost more because it comes under the category of skilled rather than operative work. They'll start calling themselves chefs and asking for a share in the profits. I want menials and that means machine work.'

'Well, you're going to have to improve it,' panted Mrs Munde. 'You can't run a business with this.'

Ham thought she was probably right and took the machine away to one of the Ark engineers. If they could power a boat surely they could improve a hamburger machine. He generously gave Mrs Munde the afternoon off. This cheered her up because she wanted to knock down her kitchen which had been oppressing her for some time. She felt the need for open spaces as she got older, perhaps so that she could look at the stars and dwell on her life. Gloria hated her mother's demolition projects and so Mrs Munde tried to do them as surreptitiously as possible, but given the nature of demolition work found that quite difficult.

She hurried home and collected her axe. 'Nasty pokey place,' she muttered. 'It's not hygenic to be confined, especially in the warm weather. I'll soon have it down,' and she started to chop at the bamboo walls.

Once upon a time her friends would have come to help her, but people had changed – or rather fridges had changed them. Mrs Munde felt that being able to store

food for longer periods had broken down the community
spirit. There was no need to share now, no need to meet
every day, gathering your veg or killing a few rabbits. The
day-to-dayness had gone out of life. Everyone lived apart
in their own little house with their own little fridges.
Noah was doing his best, but greed and iniquity were
catching up again. There had been a boom in freezer food
over the last couple of years. That was probably why
Noah had decided to launch his all-singing, all-dancing
stage-and-screen epic in a last attempt to thaw out the
world's hard and sinful heart.

Mrs Munde was so carried away with her thoughts and
her demolition that she didn't hear Gloria come home.
Gloria had decided not to move to Noah's, although the
stabling for Trebor was much better there. Taking one
look at her mother's handiwork, she swung up the ladder
into her bedroom and started to root through the trunk
that contained their vast collection of Bunny Mix ephem-
era. She found the one she wanted and squatted in an
corner, trying not to get too excited. It was called *Moonlight Over The Desert*, and had won the Purple Heart
Award for best romantic fiction. She read the blurb half-
aloud to better appreciate the sensuous prose. . . .

' "When slim brunette Naomi travels across the desert
with her uncle's caravan she doesn't expect to find true
love. A mysterious thunderstorm forces the party to take
shelter in a nomadic village, a place of sultry tradition
where she meets Roy, the most fearless camel tamer of
them all." '

The first chapter was called 'Into the desert' and, as she
read, Gloria began to sink into that semi-hypnotic state she
always experienced with Bunny Mix and her magic. . . .

'I do think, Naomi,' scolded her Aunt Ruth, 'that you
might be a bit more enthusiastic about this trip. Your
uncle has gone to a lot of trouble to arrange it for you.'

Naomi looked up from her toast, her pretty face

spoiled by a scowl. She was a slightly built girl with a weak heart, beautiful hair and piercing green eyes. Her skin glowed with the bloom of youth. Her aunt, watching her, felt a sudden twinge of envy. She remembered her own youth and her excitement at falling in love. She had told the story to her niece many times: how she had met Reuben at a cattle fair, how he had stood a head taller than any of the others, what a way he had with the heifers and what a gentleman he had been when she had fallen into the cesspit. They had walked out together for a year, then one night when the air was thick with bird song and warm rain he had asked her to marry him. She had accepted, and on their wedding night, after he had gently pulled back the sheets, she had felt a thunderclap melting her and a thick tenderness deep inside. It was like a fairy tale, and of course love is like a fairy tale, as she always told her niece.

Naomi knew what her aunt was thinking and she didn't care. She wanted to feel her own pulse beat, her own heart race. Why did they have to pack her off on a sight-seeing tour in the desert when she really wanted to go to Monte Carlo and meet a man who owned racehorses. That was the trouble with relatives; they thought they knew best. She was a headstrong young woman who liked to go fishing and make her own clothes, and although she had no idea what love could really mean she felt certain that she wasn't going to find it in the middle of the desert with her uncle.

Naomi's aunt sighed and started to clear the breakfast things. She had enough to do without worrying about her niece. There was the laundry and the dishes, and the packed lunches for her sons, and Reuben's clothes to put out, and oh, the hundred and one little things that come with marriage. She liked it, it gave her a sense of purpose.

When she had gone out of the room her niece gazed

into the mirror, trying to decide whether or not she was beautiful. She had a good figure, and was thought to be unusually intelligent, but was she beautiful? This was what she ached to know.

Soon it was time to join the caravan. She watched the servant boys swing up bales of straw and provisions. One of them caught her eye and grinned. She blushed. He had warm brown skin and a furry neck, but she would not lower herself from her class. She heard her uncle's voice: 'Naomi, are you ready? We need to be well away before dark.'

'Ready, Uncle,' she shouted, skipping towards him.

'Really,' he thought, feeling his age, 'she is lovely.'

Then they were off, rolling across the dunes as the sun spread into the glory that is the desert at dusk. Naomi sniffed the air: it was fresh and exciting. She would sleep that night dreaming of princes on well-muscled steeds.

The next day, as she ate kippers with her uncle, she noticed that he seemed preoccupied. 'What is it, Uncle Reuben?' she asked with sympathy in her voice.

'Oh, nothing I hope, just the chance of a storm. But we'll get on as quickly as we can; there's an oasis town a few miles south of here.'

Naomi felt a rush of blood. An oasis town! She had heard of them, where custom had remained unchanged for hundreds of years, and the men still carried off their brides for a honeymoon of passion behind the rocks. Long before nightfall they reached the camp, the white tents glittering and dignified under the powerful sun. 'You have to watch out for some of these chaps,' her uncle warned. 'They're friendly enough but their passions are strong. Be polite, but remember your honour.'

The chief came out from one of the tents and made signs of welcome. Naomi was thrilled. She could smell the animals, the cooking, and that different enticing scent of men in the desert. Suddenly she felt very young and asked to go and lie down. Her uncle arranged everything for her and they agreed to meet at sundown for supper. Naomi fell into a fitful sleep where she dreamed anxiously about her wardrobe. What should she wear to make an impact? Every young woman wants her first important entrance to be a success and Naomi was typical of anyone who has found themselves in a Bedouin camp without an iron. Finally, when she awoke she decided on her light silk dress specially designed to resist wrinkles. She matched it with a simple string of pearls and tied up her hair perfectly but casually. After about three hours she was satisfied that she looked as if she had made the minimum effort and achieved spectacular results. She wanted to be thought natural.

As she walked into the supper tent every eye turned to stare at her, and those admiring but uncivilised men could hardly quiet their admiration. For a few moments their whistling and lip-smacking deafened her, but her uncle bent over and told her to take it as a compliment. She noticed he seemed upset.

The meal lasted for hours, with every kind of delicacy offered to please her. At last, with the impatience of youth, she got up to take some fresh air. Once outside the tent she was overwhelmed by the menacing beauty of the desert: the timeless sand, the leering palms. She shuddered, and felt a hand against her bare shoulder.

'Forgive me.' A rich warm voice spoke. 'My name is Roy and I thought you might like some company. I am known to my tribe as a camel tamer.'

As she looked into his eyes, she knew he was more than just a passing stranger. Far away, the moon rose across acres of quiet sand. The storm had passed and the world lay still. He took her hand.

'Perhaps you would like to come to my tent? I have a fine collection of Arab weavings.'

Unable to speak she nodded her assent, and felt safe by his side as they turned from the communal dwellings into the private spaces of privilege. Naomi was used to wealth, but even she was amazed at the splendour Roy called his tent. Everywhere she saw gold and ivory and jewels without price. Roy noticed her surprise and, laughing softly, explained, 'I am more than just a camel tamer, I am also a very rich prince.'

Naomi felt inward relief. Surely now there could be no opposition to their union? But was she being too presumptuous? After all, she didn't even know if she was beautiful.

'You are the loveliest woman I have ever seen,' said Roy softly. 'Would you, perhaps, be my wife?' He waited, head bowed, not daring to look at her. He waited for at least five minutes, and still she had not answered. Bravely, he raised his eyes, and saw that she had entirely fainted away. He roused her with the scent of desert thistle, and as she regained consciousness she was saying, 'Yes, oh yes, I do so want that,' and his heart was glad.

They spent the rest of the night planning their future, lying side by side on deep cushions, but the morning brought a problem neither of them had expected. Her uncle refused his consent. Naomi fell weeping to the floor. She begged him, and promised to visit him regularly, but it was of no use. Finally, in despair, she turned to Roy and pleaded with him to make her uncle change his mind.

'I do not beg for what I want!' exclaimed Roy, and drawing his sword he chopped off Reuben's head. Naomi watched it roll away.

'You had to do it Roy, I know that, but we must send Auntie some flowers. . . .'

Gloria put down the book. She usually read on, followed Roy and Naomi into their new life together as they fearlessly crossed the desert, spurning custom and flouting convention. They were married though, so it wasn't sinful. But this time Gloria wasn't really interested. Could it be that Bunny Mix was losing her hold? Or was it perhaps a stage in her own development? She knew there were stages, three to be precise, because she had read a book by Northrop Frye that said so. Just now and again Gloria's past had been punctuated with serious literature. She had never sought it, had always had it forced upon her at station bookstalls because she was too naïve to understand that when a serious work is issued in paperback the publishers always use a misleading cover. And so she knew all about the Great Western Railway because the book cover made it look similar to *Murder on the Orient Express*; and she understood in their entirety the origins of early music because she had picked up a book that appeared to be a collection of love songs called *My Lady Neville's Lute*, with a couple intertwined round a set of musical instruments on the cover. She always read these books, even after the truth had dawned, because she was careful about money and preferred reading to making anagrams out of the railway notices.

Northrop Frye had written about the development of language through three stages: the metaphoric, where persons and matter share a common energy and are described as an inseparable unit; the didactic, where persons and matter are separate and the inner life (intellectual) assumes ascendency; and finally the prosaic, where we describe what we see and feel without recourse to imagery because we think imagining gets in the way. Gloria had enjoyed the book though she hadn't expected to, and had begun to table her own life according to its premises. And now she had clearly reached stage two, and begun to separate what she felt and what she thought.

Her musings were broken into by her mother who had noticed her daughter's presence and suggested they have a cup of tea to celebrate the end of her gloomy kitchen.

Besides, Mrs Munde wanted to talk about the Hallelujah Hamburger.

'It may get a bit chilly,' she admitted, resting the kettle over the fire, 'but I think it's nice to be in the fresh air. I don't know why we ever bothered with a kitchen at all, not a small one anyhow.'

Gloria smiled, her mind still caught up in the didactic stage of her development. As usual, Mrs Munde imagined they were communicating. She started to tell Gloria about Ham and her new role in saving the world.

'These restaurants won't be like any other,' she said proudly. 'Every dish will have a spiritual theme, so that we can think about YAHWEH while we're eating. And there won't be anything artificial, just as our Lord isn't artificial. What with the film you're making and the hamburgers I'm making, we'll have the world to rights in no time.'

'I'm not making a film, I'm collecting animals. You should know, you got me the job.' Gloria couldn't help noticing how much more fluid her sentences were becoming: she had almost reached the state of continuous prose.

Mrs Munde looked hurt. 'I've given you a start. It's up to you now. No one can say I haven't done my duty as a mother. I just hope you work hard and fall in love with the right man.'

'Why?' demanded Gloria starkly.

'Because only the right man can make you happy. Don't you long to be on the Bunny Mix Romance Show?'

'Not much.' Gloria was surprising herself again, thinking about what Desi had said about orgasms. If you could have them in supermarkets, then anything was possible. She left early, telling her mother she was out searching for a couple of bears.

When Rita and Sheila arrived, they were deep in conversation about Marlene's problem. They had spares, but not the right spare. Could they or couldn't they trim one to fit?

'What do you usually do with the – er – spares?' asked Gloria nervously. She knew she shouldn't be asking but a terrible curiosity drove her on.

Rita and Sheila glanced at one another, then Sheila said, 'You vegetarian?'

Gloria shook her head.

Sheila swallowed. 'You ever eaten sausages from a chain store called Meaty Big And Bouncy?'

Gloria nodded her head. It was the rival chain to More Meat, and usually cheaper.

'Well,' said Sheila, 'now you know what we do with the off-cuts.'

Gloria clutched her menu. Visions of sausage casserole swam before her eyes. Bevvies of sausage and mash danced in front of her. She was assaulted by hot dogs wherever she looked.

'Never mind,' said Rita cheerily. 'You'll know what to avoid now. It's all part of life's rich tapestry.'

Gloria didn't think so. Mrs Munde had always claimed you are what you eat. What did that make Gloria? Could she truthfully say on her wedding night that she'd never had a man inside her? More and more Gloria wondered whether there would ever be a wedding night.

No one noticed her tumult because Marlene had arrived and was clearly anxious to hear the decision.

'We can do it, but you'll have to come for a fitting.'

Marlene sighed. 'I knew I could trust you.'

'And afterwards you go for a complete rest.'

'Yes, I'll book in at a rest home and take the healing waters, even though it will mean missing the early days of filming – and I so wanted to see you three in your costumes. I'm so happy girls, I truly am,' and she kissed everyone goodbye and set off for the bus.

'Filming's been brought forward, Gloria,' Desi announced. 'They'll want you on set tomorrow to help

with the crocodiles. Noah's determined to do the big
scenes in one take and rehearse the extras last.'

'But I haven't collected any animals yet.'

'We don't want them all at once. It'll be bad enough
when we have to go on tour in that smelly ship. I've told
Noah we want a private cruiser. Why he has to tour it
beats me. He could just release the movie.'

'You know what he feels about personal appearances,'
said Sheila. 'He believes that the ordinary housewife and
the average man in the street need something bright and
exciting to polish up their dull grey lives. Besides, we're
booked out everywhere; it's going to make a fortune. This
is the biggest theatre spectacle anyone has ever seen, and
it's got Bunny Mix doing the screenplay and YAHWEH
himself helping with the dialogue. How can it fail – the
winner of the Purple Heart Award and the Creator of the
world brought together for the first time under the direction of one of society's most controversial and charismatic
leaders who hasn't been seen in public for fourteen years.'

'Hey, that's very good,' admired Rita.

Sheila blushed. 'It's what I've written for the press
release.' She went on: 'Look, why don't we all have a
Nineveh deep-dish and talk about our lives. Gloria, we
hardly know anything about you.'

Gloria knew that Sheila wanted to be kind but she felt
it was too soon in her personal reconstruction to talk
about Northrop Frye and what she suspected was happening to her. Suppose they laughed? Making the excuse that
she must go and help her mother demolish the kitchen,
she left. Desi, she realised, didn't believe her, but she
could always explain later.

By the time she got home her mother had already
started on the parlour as well as the kitchen, and Gloria
wondered how the bedrooms were staying up. 'Willpower,' said Mrs Munde in an offhand manner. 'If I want
the bedrooms to stay up, they stay up. I built them,
they're part of my life.'

Gloria realised that there are advantages to being in the first, or metaphoric, stage of development. Her mother made no distinction between thinking things and objects of thought, and so appeared to maintain an extraordinary degree of control over her environment.

'Her control is instinctual, though,' thought Gloria piously. 'When I regain control, it will be conscious.'

Such smugness nearly always accompanies second-stage development. Gloria now no longer trusted her instincts; she was looking for clues and isolating experience. In her case this was a good and necessary thing, because she had read the whole of Northrop Frye and knew that there was somewhere else to move on to when she was satisfied with her separateness. This didn't stop her being tedious though, as Doris noted when they met the following day.

Doris had seen a lot of development in her time and she wasn't excited about Gloria's, just mentioned it casually while she waxed the stage set to resemble a place without form, and void.

'I see you're in the second stage,' she sniffed.

Gloria was startled. How did Doris know? She'd only met her once.

'Well, you seem more purposeful this morning; something about your stride, the way you hold your head, and you've already asked me five questions in half an hour.'

'Have I?' replied Gloria, incredulous.

'Six now, and not one of them about love. It's a dead giveaway. 'Course you were in a fallen state before, not a real metaphoric state.'

'What do you mean?' demanded Gloria, offended.

'I mean you weren't poetic before, just sloppy, so it's a good thing you've pulled yourself out of it. Nothing gives poetry a worse name than people who talk drivel, and try and pretend it's got an inner meaning because it's about flowers and love and things. Poetry's got muscle, you were all flab,' and Doris made a disgusted noise with her top teeth.

Gloria was ashamed; she hadn't realised that Doris could be so astute. But then she was an organic philosopher with a wealth of life as it is lived behind her. Gloria decided to be humble.

'It's the romantic fiction that does it. I've never really read anything else, except what I've picked up by accident.' And she explained how she was often duped at station bookstalls. 'But I do know those Bunny Mix love letters off by heart. They're different.'

Doris agreed they were; then Gloria told her how her mother was making the bedrooms stay up through sheer willpower. 'And she's much worse about romantic fiction than I am, so how does she do it?'

Doris considered. 'She must have a hobby that saves her. Is she interested in anything else?'

Gloria mentioned the stars, and Doris looked pleased.

'That's it then: she's joined herself to the great cosmos. Why don't you try and get her to do a degree?'

Gloria shuddered. If her mother made the second stage too she might take over the world.

'I've got to get a move on,' panted Doris. 'They want this set ready for the Creation scene.'

A group of burly men came by wheeling lights. One of them addressed Gloria. 'They want you down with the crocodiles. We've got to make this place look like a swamp in chaos.'

Gloria followed his directions, ending up at the swiming pool. Rita and Sheila were already there drinking Piña Coladas even though it was hardly past breakfast time. Gloria sighed. This was the life she had read about. How typical that she should discover it when she no longer cared.

Desi was getting into a suit of what looked like designer chain mail. She grinned at Gloria. 'They've cast me as the warlike one. I've got to tell the great Unpronounceable what a shit he's being, destroying the happy pagan order and returning us all to the soil so that he can create the world in his own image.'

Gloria thought back to what she knew about the book of Genesis. There was an explanation on the pagan gods, then a denouncement about how undemocratic they were, then a blood scene where everyone went to war and YAHWEH destroyed the mystically created world and redid it himself in colours he preferred. Then, like a gentleman, he withdrew as gently as possible until the new world had made such a mess of things he decided to intervene again, this time using Noah as an assistant. It was good box office material, providing the pagan world wasn't made to seem too attractive or sympathetic.

'Sheila's got to wear a false nose,' said Desi, picking it out of the prop box. 'We can't be too glamorous.'

Someone came running by with a clapperboard. 'To your places please, in costume please, the director's on his way.'

Rita, Sheila and Desi stood arrogantly under the orange tree that was to symbolise their womanhood. The first scene was entirely theirs. They were to make rude remarks about the Unpronounceable and complain a lot about their dwindling powers. Gloria suddenly realised that she was going to see Noah in the flesh for the first time. She sat respectfully by the crocodiles and watched the pathway up to the house. What she saw was a spherical man with a bright bald head. He was around four feet tall with the blackest, most piercing eyes possible in anything other than a crow. As he walked down towards the pool all the hired hands and technicians bowed and murmured their admiration. The figure appeared not to notice; his gaze fastened on his daughters-in-law under the orange tree.

'You're too pretty,' he shouted. 'Can't we get a wig or some false teeth?'

The costume department looked blank. They didn't have either, though they could get them by the afternoon.

But Noah wanted to shoot now. 'I need the light,' he
complained. 'Just look at this light.'

Gloria looked and it was just the same as on any other
morning, but then she wasn't artistic.

Noah was talking again. 'Who's got a wig? I know one
of you lot at least must be wearing a wig. Let me have it,
come on, let's have a wig for the Lord. It's not much to
ask. He made you all, so why not give him something
back. Give me a wig.' He was very strong when he spoke,
and soon he had three wigs at his feet. 'Thank you, Lord.'
He raised his hands to heaven. 'I see the Lord is with us
today. He's here on this film set, opening up your hearts
to his love.' The three wigless ones felt comforted and
blushed, but Noah hadn't finished. 'Who's got some teeth?
Let me have some teeth for his greater glory. Praise him
and give me your teeth. You'll get them back, and the
Lord himself will have blest them.' One of the cameramen
offered his top set (he never wore the bottoms when he
was working), then another his gold-crowned dentures.
'Thank you brothers,' crooned Noah. 'I know the Lord
will bless you in your endeavours today and I promise
you that after this whatever you chew in his name will
never make your belly ache.' From the lofty pinnacle of
her second stage Gloria was detached enough to admire
Noah's way with words. She was glad she didn't have
any removable parts to offer, and for the first time she
understood her mother just a little. Mrs Munde had been
in Noah's company for fourteen years. No wonder she
couldn't distinguish between subject and object when even
her teeth might be whisked out for the glory of the Lord.
Noah went over to the orange tree and set about making
Rita, Sheila and Desi as ugly as possible. Sheila didn't like
it but there was nothing she could do.

'You told me this was going to make me a star,' she
moaned. 'If I'd known I was going to be treated like this I
would have asked for an advance.'

'I already did,' said Desi through her chain mail. 'You know what he's like.'

'Yeah, but I always forget until I see him again,' sighed Sheila.

When they were particularly hideous Noah decided to start filming. 'I see a lot of similarities here to *Macbeth*, don't you?' Gloria overheard one of the art people say. 'The grouping, the thematic construction of their dialogue, the portents contained in the most casual sentences. . . ?'

'You're right, you're right. It's very much folk tale rather than myth, isn't it?'

'Hold on,' said Gloria, butting in and so scoring another personal first. 'This is the inspired word of God, isn't it? As delivered to Noah in a mighty cloud of printed leaflets?'

The pair looked at her blankly. 'You think all this is God's idea? What would the creator of the world be doing on a film set?'

'Perhaps he wants the publicity,' replied Gloria tartly. She hated intellectuals. They just smiled at her and wandered off. Gloria called after them, 'If you're so smart why have you got dandruff?'

Perhaps it was Gloria's presumptuous confidence, or perhaps just the sight of Noah collecting his wigs that caused the cosmic cloud to hover over the film set just at that moment. No one noticed, because the superbeings inside wanted to disguise themselves as an innocent bit of weather. But there was a riot going on. Things with wings and lyres begged the Unpronounceable for mercy, but not much was forthcoming.

'I want his ass!' thundered YAHWEH. 'He's gone too far this time. I never said I'd work on his filthy film. I never said I'd work with that woman either, that rabbit woman. What does he think I am?'

'Destroy him, destroy him,' urged one of the more hyperactive angels.

'I can't do that,' snapped God. 'It would mean a riot.
I've just started to get some control down there, and our
Good Food Guide's selling well. I like being in print. I
just don't want to be taken for granted. I have my feelings
too. Now who's going to think of a plan?'

Lucifer put his hand up. 'Why don't you negotiate?
Arrange to meet him, threaten a bit, frighten him, tell him
he's got to stop filming.'

'No, no.' YAHWEH was getting exasperated. 'I *want* to
be toured in York and Wakefield. It's not his ideas I hate,
it's the way he moves. What's the plot of this thing
anyway?'

Patiently one of the angels explained, and a strange
gleam came into the Unpronounceable's eye. 'An ocean-
going ark, eh? That might be fun. Lucifer, tell that skunk-
sized little baldy I want a meeting, right after his press
reception next week. Tell him we'll land at the Gaza Strip
and he'd better be there.'

Lucifer shot off, leaving the Lord a trifle calmer.
Relieved, the angels went back to their hymn books.

When the crew had a steak break Gloria walked home to
see how her mother was getting on. New understandings
bring new responsibilities, and Gloria felt it was her duty
to protect her mother from her own excesses and any
possibility of further evolution. Her mother had erected
something that resembled a beach party windbreak in the
space where the kitchen had been. She was experimenting
with Noah's machine for the Hallelujah Hamburger.
When Gloria saw the extent and folly of the device she
told Mrs Munde very firmly to leave it alone.

'I can't,' declared her mother, trying to help the machine
out of its self-imposed labour. Finally she delivered a
reasonably shaped quarterpounder. 'The problem is that
the burgers get stuck in the funnel and I have to squeeze
them out. It's messy work, but it's for His Glory.'

'Why don't you tell him to stick to vegetarian food?'

'He's being guided by the Unpronounceable, that's why. He doesn't tell God how to run a small business. Besides, meat's popular. He's always been involved in meat.'

When Mrs Munde decided to be on someone's side, that was it for ever and ever. What they did wasn't her concern; it only concerned her that she should defend them. She had never heard of mixed feelings. There were friends and there were enemies. As far as it mattered to her, Ham could be making mudpies to sell on Goodwin Sands. She liked him and he wanted her to help. That was enough.

Gloria knew her mother wasn't going to be persuaded so she thought she'd go for a swim instead. It was hot and she had a hard afternoon ahead, knowing nothing about crocodiles. She ran through the bushes and plunged headfirst into the clear water of the river. It was green and cold and slippery with fish. She caught a fat one between her teeth, beat it to death on a stone and took it back to her mother.

Mrs Munde smiled and put it in the fish kettle. 'A young girl like you with a future shouldn't do tomboy things like that.'

'I wanted to give you a present,' said Gloria, a bit upset.

'I wasn't being critical,' soothed Mrs Munde. 'I just wish you'd use a rod, that's all.' The two of them sat in silence, then Mrs Munde remembered her news. 'We've been invited to a special supper to celebrate the start of the new Bunny Mix Romance Show. You see how useful it is to work in high places? It's tomorrow night, up at the house, and you must do something about your hair. I'm having a new dress made.'

Gloria's heart sank. What could be worse than having to accompany her mother to a supper full of media people? Perhaps she could invent a headache. Back on set that afternoon she told Desi her woes.

'I know,' said Desi. 'I sent the invitation.'

Gloria had a relapse and couldn't think of anything to say, but Desi smiled. 'I wanted you to see the world. You haven't done much, after all.'

'Why?' asked Gloria suspiciously. 'There's no such thing as a free lunch.'

'I see you've reached the second stage. Well, that's too bad. I like a bit of romantic nonsense.' Desi turned away, then called back: 'You'd be surprised how easy it is to find out about people, but come anyway. You can meet Bunny Mix.'

Again it was typical and tedious. All her life she'd wanted to meet that famous rabbit of romance, and now she had it on a plate and was just about to turn vegetarian. Well, perhaps she should try and stomach it, for the sake of her development as a fully rounded person. Desi was odd, and Gloria wasn't altogether sure that she liked her. Or maybe she liked her a lot. Both were reasons to back away. She decided to go and ask Doris about the nature of affection, but Doris had been put to work on a papier-mâché heathen temple and didn't have time to be metaphysical. . . .

The following evening, servants lit the pathway to the house with a thousand flares. Anybody who was anybody was expected at the reception. Gloria walked in silence beside her mother, hardly daring to look at her. Mrs Munde's dress, while being a single creation, could be seen as two parts because each half appeared to do entirely different things to her body. Above, the sculptured bodice crushed her breasts into firm pineapple shapes; below, the flourishing skirt, too generous for a woman with girth, made her hips spread like marmalade on a hot day. It was all crimson with little white roses for decoration.

But Gloria needn't have worried. Her mother was not overdressed, nor was she out of place. Sheila was almost

bent double underneath the gold she had managed to attach to every spare inch of flesh. Japeth, whose shoulders were almost as wide as the door he was leaning against and whose ears stood out at right angles to his close-cropped head, seemed to be wearing a body suit covered in platinum fish scales. As for Desi, Gloria chose to ignore the expanses of bare brown skin she had decided to leave undressed. She concentrated on Shem, who was much smaller than his brothers, with masses of curly hair. Was it his own? 'Don't even think about it,' she told herself. Out of the corner of her eye, Gloria could see her mother talking to Ham. He was at least a foot taller and made Mrs Munde look all the more like a billiard ball.

So this was it, this was what all the magazines talked about; this was Society, the rich and beautiful all in one place. 'How many of them are on drugs?' she wondered. 'How many of them have unusual sexual habits?' Then she blushed as she remembered what Desi had said about thinking about *it*. She had begun to. Did that mean she was soon to . . . Quickly she banished the idea, but she couldn't help going pink.

'So what are you thinking about, standing here alone?' Desi was there with a bottle of champagne in her hand, offering some to Gloria.

'Oh, I was just thinking what a nice time I'm having.' Gloria discovered she had also learnt to lie. It was useful, this second stage.

'You could have a better time if you wanted,' hinted Desi meaningfully.

Gloria collected herself. Was she about to be offered illicit substances or was she . . . ? She coughed.

Desi looked straight at her. 'Why not get drunk with me?'

'I can't,' said Gloria. 'I'm with my mother. She'll get upset and you can't begin to understand what that means.' Desi shrugged and smiled and Gloria watched her lean body and embarrassingly tightly clad bottom swing away across the room. She supposed that Desi would be called attractive, and she momentarily cursed Doris for not having been willing to talk that afternoon. She couldn't be expected to find out about instinct and impulse and the nature of attraction all by herself. Just as she was about to become tearful with frustration, Gross Reality intruded in the devastating, show-stopping shape of that rabbit of romance, Bunny Mix herself.

Down either side of the hall the crowds parted, and as if by magic conversation stopped. Then came Bunny, smooth as if she were on castors, gliding down towards Noah who stood at the other end of the red carpet like a small sacrifice. Her face was very pale and her eyes were very black. A gash of brilliant red marked her mouth, while the finest emeralds explained which of her was neck and which was not. About her ankles three little dogs gambolled in matching sailor suits. When the famous novelist reached Noah she engulfed him in a maze of taffeta and button pearls. There was a muffled shriek which the company took to be an acknowledgement of Bunny's hug, then everyone cheered and the novelist unclamped herself, taking her place as guest of honour at the top of the table. Inspired by a stroke of wickedness or benevolence, Desi had placed Gloria and Mrs Munde very near the great pair and Mrs Munde of course was close to dying from a surfeit of pleasure. Gloria sat down by Desi and asked for some help in deciphering the cutlery.

About halfway through the soup, Mrs Munde started to question Bunny about her novels. How did she always manage to be so wonderfully accurate in her interpretations of the passions? How could she see into the heart of ordinary people and show them the truth about love?

Bunny gave a little laugh. 'Well, dear, the true artist is more than just flesh and blood. The true artist is the bearer of wisdom down the annals of time. I have been given a gift, and I believe it is a gift from God, to explore the passions with you all, so that we can learn together how to tame and control that mighty and terrifying force. You see, artists have visions and dream dreams. They are the keepers of society's conscience, the guiding light on a rough and stormy way. Take my show, my Romance Show. I can't tell you how many people that show has helped – people who thought they were unloved and unwanted and then, through me, have gained a new confidence. A woman should be sent flowers every day. What I'm talking about is pure and holy love. I have no time for the kind of salacious rubbish put out by others who call themselves romantic writers.'

Bunny Mix coughed and no one dared mention the name of Jackie Colic, her arch rival who had actually said in public that she thought the keeper of the holy tryst was a fat fraud who had probably never had an orgasm in her life.

'I've always wanted to know how the true artist works,' pursued Mrs Munde, 'but you don't get to meet many when you're busy in the kitchen all day.'

'Well, no,' sympathised Bunny. 'You wouldn't because the true artist is always rich. I have no patience with those who toil away in squalor, claiming to develop new art forms. The experimental novel is a waste of public funds, and I'm sure Noah would agree with me.' (Noah did.) 'The important thing is to create for the people and then the people will buy it, which is what I do. It's very selfish not to think of your reading public. I am rich because I provide a valuable public service. Yes, I do, but the Nineveh Council don't offer *me* a grant.' She gave another trill and reached for the salmon mousse.

'Bunny,' put in Shem from across the table, 'some people call you the founder of romantic fiction. Do you think that's true?'

The rabbit of romance blushed and dabbed at her red gash mouth with her napkin. 'No, I'm not a woman to take credit where it isn't due. You see, I am the heiress, the interpreter of the women who first inspired us. I mean, of course, those three sisters who used to live with their drug-crazed brother in a desolate mango swamp round Ilkley. I have taken on their burden, and I like to think I have made it a little more accessible.'

'But they weren't rich,' threw in Desi.

'No dear, they were socialists. I can't help that.'

'But you were going to tell us how you work,' said Mrs Munde eagerly, and settled back thinking that Heaven must be like this. Bunny shuffled and took a deep breath. 'I get up each morning at five a.m. because I don't need much sleep and I take a walk in the garden. If it rains, one of my servants carries an umbrella. I always sniff the mint at half past five because it's so heavenly. Then, at six o'clock, I have breakfast: honey and wholemeal toast and a cup of dandelion coffee. Then I spend at least half an hour in the toilet, because you can't do your best work on a full bowel. I always keep a copy of *Vague* in the toilet because they do have such nice clothes, and it helps me forget about the poor who are always writing me letters asking me to help them improve their wretched condition. I have to write back and tell them they never will be better off because it takes money to be young and beautiful. They can, however, stay hard-working, clean and inviting to their equals. I console them with this. At eight o'clock I read my fan mail which is then sent off to be recycled into trees. I am, you see, a great supporter of ecology and I've just sent off an article to *Vague* showing how the poor are ruining our environment because they use so much wood keeping their fires going. Well, after I've read my mail I sit down on my specially padded pink sofa and dictate my book. I like to wear eye-shades and slippers while I do this, and sometimes I drink champagne because the artist has a right to be comfortable, suffering as we do in inner ways. We give of ourselves you see. I dictate my novel for three hours fifty minutes precisely, then I have my maid put out my swimming costume. I do two lengths of breaststroke – so important for a woman – and two lengths of doggy paddle, then I hook myself onto my pink winch – it was a present from my fans – and Oscar winds me back onto land. The rest of the day I spend finding new recipes for my cookbooks or talking to friends.'

'Fascinating,' murmured all the guests who were lucky enough to have heard this saga.

Noah stood up. He was wearing a red-and-white spotted bow tie. 'I'd like to offer my personal thanks to Bunny and all that she stands for. We've known each other a long time and her support has always made my life easier. She's on the Glory Train, brothers and sisters, and all of us here tonight are going to see some big changes in our lives as the Unpronounceable takes control.'

No one knew that Noah's speech was as much motivated by anxiety as it was by genuine affection. Just before the meal he'd got the message from Lucifer about YAHWEH wanting a meeting and he felt uncomfortable. His fame and fortune depended on the Unpronounceable remaining cooperative.

It was late. Gloria and Mrs Munde walked home together, and Mrs Munde talked about the stars:

'I sometimes fancy that my body is made up of all the different stars. Leo's in my chest; I'm sure it's Leo because my heart roars. I've always had a roaring heart. Whatever I'm feeling my heart is roaring inside. I don't think I'll die, I think I'll combust. One day my frame will be too weak and my banging heart too strong and the lion will be out, gone, escaped, leaving me here in a little heap. Still, I'd rather it was that way than have no lion at all. Modern people, they don't feel much, Gloria, they do all they can not to get excited, not to get upset. . . .'

Gloria was confused. Since she had begun to think, she had come to see her mother as very complex indeed. Before, she had seen her in cartoon terms: larger than life, which she probably was, and entirely fixed in her ideas.

How could a woman who wallowed in romantic fiction and who believed in the power of the Unpronounceable be so affected by, and so affect, her environment? Perhaps Doris was right; perhaps her astronomy did give her a dimension that made her poetic rather than just prosaic, so the rest of her world condemned her to be. Then Gloria thought about herself. Until her epiphany with Northrop Frye she'd been an emotional amoeba. Now she had split into two and could observe herself developing – but that didn't solve the problem of her mother, who appeared to carry round all her contradictions without needing to examine them.

Mrs Munde was still talking. 'I love the stars because they calm me down. When I look at them I feel like I'm looking into myself, myself without all the cares of the world. The lion sleeps then, but only then. Even when it's cloudy I can tell just where everything is. We've been together for years. As I get older they don't seem so far away, but perhaps that's because I know more about them. Look, it's a clear night; I'll show you what's what,' and Mrs Munde gave Gloria a guided tour of the heavenly bodies. For the first time Gloria saw how beautiful they were. Her mother made patterns, showed her how to join up the giant dots, so that the sky was no longer full of disparate elements but instead seemed more of a shorthand or a music score left by someone who wanted others to make an effort too. No wonder they didn't seem far away. Something you love is never far away because you know it so well, because it has become part of you. Mrs Munde had absorbed the stars and she believed that the stars inhabited her. What matter if it were true or not? – perhaps it wasn't literally true, but it was true enough. Gross Reality is intrusive enough without our help; there is no need to ruin poetry simply to emphasise it.

Doris had been right about one thing, certainly: Gloria's previous state had been blurred. She had been a blender for every possible feeling, but that didn't make her poetic,

only muddled. She had lacked her mother's primitive
unity; she only had her mother's rather confused associ-
ations with romance and the soul and the great mysterious
outdoors. Perhaps passion does dilute with generations.
Mrs Munde redeemed her own worst excesses because
she was a colossus; her kitchen and parlour were too
small for her soul, and if she was misguided in seeking the
kitchens of the world via the Hallelujah Hamburger at
least she was still seeking. For eighteen years Gloria had
sought nothing and absorbed everything; her soul had
been without form and void. Maybe it wasn't her fault:
living with a colossus, however flawed or deranged, is a
tiring business, and she had only found her store of extra
energy by accident. Mrs Munde, like all true primal forces,
never realised the effect she had on other people and was
always bewildered when friends confessed they found her
a bit much. Presumably they were worried that her resi-
dent lion might make a break for it all over them.

'They're steadfast, stars are,' Mrs Munde said. 'Even
though they move across the sky and planets don't, I
think stars have the advantage. A star can travel and still
be fixed because it knows its orbit. It knows where it
belongs. That's why stars are so important to travellers.
I'll tell you a tale.

'Once there was a traveller who put on stout boots to
wander the world because he felt it had a secret he didn't
know. After some time he met an old woman gathering
firewood and he helped the woman, being well brought
up. She offered him shelter for the night and promised to
answer a question, should he wish to ask one. The young
man thought for a while and then he said, "Do you know
the secret of the world?" "Yes," she replied, "the secret of
the world is so simple, it could be written on a blade of
grass with the juice of a berry. You will find it if you
study the stars. To study the stars you do not need a
telescope."

'The young man was confused, but he didn't press the

old woman who clearly had better things to do than go on communicating. He set off again, travelling through distant lands where he found many marvels and some happiness, but still he felt restless. He hadn't found what he was searching for. One summer night he came to a temple where a girl of his own age was laying out vessels for a ceremony. Out of politeness he asked if he could help her. She was grateful and suggested he might stay with her that night and she would answer him one question if he chose to ask. As they sat by the fire, he entertained her with his stories and then he said, "But I am looking for the secret of the world. Do you know what it is?"

'The girl laughed. "Stand against the door and put a mark where your head reaches." The young man did as she said. "Now," explained the girl, "the secret lies in the space you have just made. From head to foot in your own space the secret lies, and if you still do not understand, go and look at the stars." The young man was confused, but clearly the girl had better things to do than go on explaining. He slept, and in the morning departed with his curiosity all the stronger.

'Months passed and the young man grew a beard. He visited fabulous towns made from cobwebs and walked in places that only animals had seen before. He loved the world more and more but still he had not found what he was looking for. At last he came to a humble village by a river, and at the river he met a woman washing. Being thoughtful, he offered to help her carry her bundle back to her home, and she invited him to stay the night and promised to answer a question if he wished to ask. The young man sighed, and told the woman about his trip and the people who had already advised him. "Both of them told me to look at the stars, and one also told me that the secret lay in myself. But I am travelling the world because the secret lies outside myself. I follow it and it gets further away."

'The woman was sorry for the man and gave him a bowl of soup. Then she explained, "The secret of the world is this: the world is entirely circular and you will go round and round endlessly, never finding what you want, unless you have found what you really want inside yourself. When you follow a star you know you will never reach that star; rather it will guide you to where you want to go. It's a reference point, not an end in itself, even though you seem to be following it. So it is with the world. It will only ever lead you back to yourself. The end of all your exploring will be to cease from exploration and know the place for the first time." The young man thanked her and in the morning set out for home.

'That's the thing,' said Mrs Munde. 'Knowing your orbit, like they do. They don't drift, they travel, but they always move back to their original place.'

'I thought you could never go back,' said Gloria, dredging up a bit of philosophy she'd seen in some magazine. 'What about progress?'

'Progress is a mixed bag,' her mother told her. 'Some things get better, but some things get a lot worse, it seems to me. Besides, if you've dropped a stitch somewhere in the jumper of life, you have to pick it up again or your pattern will come out lopsided.'

If Mrs Munde had been able, she would have told Gloria that progress is not linear, and that only the very stupid associate what is primitive with what is outmoded. As it was, she talked instead about the jumper of life, which we don't much want to listen to as it is rather a sentimental regression after her first and pertinent point about dropped stitches. While she continues we can talk among ourselves.

Just as a point of interest: the Bible is probably the most anti-linear text we possess, which is why it's such a joy. People have believed for centuries, on the authority of the book of Genesis, that there was once a deluge over the whole world. Maybe Genesis is less important than it was, but we still like flood stories – whether they're Plato's Atlantis or yarns about the Loch Ness monster. Freud says we are preoccupied with deluges as a safeguard against bed-wetting. This may or may not be true; what remains true is the potency of the myth. Myths hook and bind the mind because at the same time they set the mind free: they explain the universe while allowing the universe to go on being unexplained; and we seem to need this even now, in our twentieth-century grandeur. The Bible writers didn't care that they were bunching together sequences some of which were historical, some preposterous, and some downright manipulative. Faithful recording was not their business; faith was. They set it out in order to create a certain effect, and did it so well that we're still arguing about it. Every believer is an anarchist at heart. True believers would rather see governments topple and history rewritten than scuff the cover of their faith. For them, all things are possible. They are poets, insomuch as poetry expands, whereas prose defines. Believers are dangerous and mad and may even destroy the world in a different deluge if they deem it necessary to keep the faith. They are fanatics, and reasonable people will never deal with their excesses until reasonable people find a counter-myth in themselves and learn to fight fire with fire. It's very potent, that Punch and Judy show book. The Romantics didn't need it because they found their own fire; but almost every other quasi-revolt has gone back to it, because when the heart revolts it wants outrageous things that cannot possibly be factual. Robes and incense and larger-than-life and miracles and heroes. It's all there, it's heart-food, and the more we deprive ourselves of colours and folly, the more attractive that now legitimate folly will become.

But read it; read it for its arrogance, its sleight of hand. It's very beautiful, and it's a pointer for living. The mistake

is to use it as a handbook. That way madness lies. When
Mrs Munde delivered herself into the everlasting hands of
the Almighty she did so because her heart was too loud
for this muffled world. She was out of place. She loved
the stars and she had no one to talk to; she found romance
and it wasn't enough. She was not free-thinking in a sense
that would have allowed her to question the institutions
that made her moody: her family, her marriage, her career
prospects. Suddenly she was offered a choice that gave
her the space to be safe and eccentric at the same time.
She took it, and the mind gave way a little – as minds do
in the face of a massive compromise that can't be articu-
lated. She's soggy round the edges and peculiar in her
outlook but her heart is still loud; and to keep the roaring
inside, however you do it, must be worth something.

Gloria sighed. As yet she hadn't had a calling and so she
didn't know the power that involved. She didn't know
that on the wild nights no one can call you home except
the one who knows your name. For Mrs Munde the wild
nights came very often, her lion heart being what it was.
She couldn't risk not reaching home again; and so if the
Lord could bring her home, and the Lord wanted her to
make hamburgers, she was going to do it. It seemed to
her like a bargain.

They fell into silence until they reached home. Gloria
thought of going to bed. She wanted to touch her mother,
but that was such a new feeling she decided to leave it
until another time. There might not be any Gross Reality
around to save them if it started to go wrong. Mrs Munde
said she was going to stay up and read *Genesis* again.

'The film won't be as good as the book,' she sighed.
'They never are.'

Gloria just smiled. She didn't care about the film. It
was a means to an end as far as she was concerned – her
own ends, her own development.

'I'll see you for breakfast. We can eat my fish.'

Once in her hammock Gloria fell instantly asleep, and dreamed that she was walking through a valley of stars that all seemed very close until she tried to touch them. One star she wanted more than the others, and followed it for many miles until she came to a lake. Exhausted, she sat down and noticed that the star was sitting down too, but in the water. Laughing she got up and plunged in to catch it, but it broke in her hands. Each time she tried to catch it it broke again, but when she sat beside it, it stayed whole. She looked up and saw that it was really in the sky and its image in the water. She didn't understand. Then at her elbow she heard a tapping and it was the orange demon.

'What's going on?' she demanded.

'It's your first lesson in plural reality,' it said, and vanished.

Doris was in a bad mood. She had been hired as a cleaner and now they wanted her to take on a bit-part as an unbelieving crone. It wasn't especially demanding, just involved wearing old clothes and shaking her fist a lot as the great Unpronounceable tried to force everyone to repent, and when they didn't – false gods being difficult to give up – he would destroy them. Doris didn't like what she'd seen of the script. She knew it was a famous adaptation by the rabbit of romance, but she preferred the original which had some human drama and more than a touch of grand hyperbole. Noah and his cosmic friend had a way with words that Bunny lacked. She kept trying to make the thing progress – first there was this, then that, then the conclusion. In the original *Genesis* or *How I Did It*, events, people and places had been lumped together purely for dramatic effect. Doris admired that; it showed a magnificent lack of concern for order and common sense. She wasn't a believer herself because she didn't like mixing politics with poetry, and she felt that Noah had gone too far, trying to take over the world and change everything. He should have been content to stay a cult figure and write extravagant best sellers. She wondered how much his sons had influenced him, and whether his retirement was more to do with letting them get on with it. That was probably it, she thought, given how pushy they all were. And the wives; if only they could have a nasty accident in a dark place.

Doris was old enough to remember the time when Noah had made his first announcement about the One True God on board *Nightqueen*. The cloud trick had been the clincher. However had he persuaded the Creator of the universe to appear in a fluorescent cloud and do some fancy sky writing? He deserved to be successful with contacts like that. Then there had been the Glory Crusade and the move towards a religious and political coup. Maybe it had done some good, helped a few people, but she still felt it a pity that someone who had such a way with words should turn out to be a lousy fascist bastard.

Noah was right wing, suspicious of women and totally committed to money as a medium for communication. Yet when he spoke he charmed. He could transform his audiences' dull grey lives for an hour or two. Doris had been to most of those meetings, and when she came out she realised she had been conned and seduced because most of what he implied was dangerous nonsense. But while she was inside she believed him. He became a focus for pain and disappointment, urged his audience to lay their burden down and rest in him, told them they'd see their country become great again, painted a bright future for their children. It was all colour with Noah. Not surprising then, that many wanted to keep the feeling. He had created a congregation who wanted to look after one another. For some reason, this was their first experience of family. It meant they had friends to call on, resources to claim and, most important, that they would never be alone again. The sinister side lay in their attitude to those who didn't believe. If you refused the message you were an outcast, and although they might claim to love your soul the rest of you could literally and metaphorically go to hell. Doris objected to this. Why should a God of love disown a large part of his beloved? Noah said that love is hard and strong and love makes choices. Love discriminates and above all, love cannot embrace the inherently unlovely, ie those without YAHWEH in their hearts. They might feel concern and patience perhaps, but only for a time. 'Live in the light,' said Noah. 'Know your enemies.'

Then there was his preoccupation with frozen food. This was some kind of personal oddity, but why make it a tenet of his doctrine? No believer was supposed to eat frozen food, and no believer was allowed to own a fridge because Noah felt it flouted the life process of freshness, decay and death. It was, he said, flying in the face of nature. Doris loved her fridge: her pots of cottage cheese, her smoked ham, and in the freezer she kept Black Forest Gâteau, Noah's particular anathema. She wondered why he'd hired her even to do the cleaning. Surely he could tell. She imagined the telltale smell of refrigerated food sticking to her clothes. But then, people in power – rulers, fanatics, TV personalities – always made a virtue out of their peculiarities; bow ties, a passion for oysters or silk knickers, and soon you had the whole world clamouring to dress up or make themselves sick. 'Heroes,' she mused. 'Why does the world need heroes?'

'Obvious,' said the orange demon, poking its head round her duster. 'The impulse to worship is impossible to eradicate. Even the most prosaic have to worship something.'

'What are you doing here?' demanded Doris. 'I thought you were on holiday.'

'I was. I've come back because there's work to do. I've got a new client, that friend of yours, Gloria. We couldn't leave her like she was, could we?'

'What's she need you for? She's been reading Northrop Frye.'

'I'm teaching her to be poetic while she teaches herself to be analytic. She used to be a jar of instant whip, you know.'

'I know that. I've seen it all before – the move towards reason, the loss of wonder, the empty place in the heart. I'm an organic philosopher, remember.'

'Yes,' replied the demon patiently, 'but if we don't give her something real to worship she'll end up like her mother. An emotional vacuum is a dangerous thing. You said yourself we all need heroes,' and the demon started to slide up and down Doris' polished floor.

'You leave off that floor. I've just done it. Besides, I've got my own worries. They want me in this film.'

'Doesn't matter about the film,' shouted the demon from the other end of the room. 'We're not interested in plot, are we?'

'You might not be,' grumbled Doris, 'but I am. This may be my one appearance in print. I may never occur in another novel. You appear all the time; you can afford to be relaxed.'

It was true. The orange Thing turns up everywhere, as a demon, a sprite, omnipotent author, flashes of insight. It is there in *Jude the Obscure*, *The Little Foxes*; it probably impersonated Scarlett O'Hara in most of *Gone with the Wind*. Whenever something other than the plot drops in, it is really the orange demon adding an extra dimension.

The demon did a twirl and sailed back to where Doris was standing, arms folded, looking like a brush with her thin body and tufted head.

'We're going to have trouble with this flood myth stuff. I know it's supposed to have happened a long time ago — if it happened at all — and I know we're only making a movie, but have you ever known someone to have the power and not use it?' and with a bright flash, the creature was gone.

'I hate them elementals,' spat Doris. 'Always popping up being cryptic and pretending they're doing you a favour. "Flood myths", what's all that about anyway . . . ?'

When Gloria woke up the sun was streaming through her window. She could hear her mother clattering about with the pots and pans down in the windbreak, a smell of fish rising on the breeze. She slithered down the rope and poured herself a cup of tea. 'There's a note for you here,' said Mrs Munde. 'I've got to get up to the house, so I'll leave you to it,' and she put on her hat and coat and disappeared. Gloria slit the envelope and saw the gilded Noah crest. There was an address inside, a train timetable and instructions on how to find her destination from the station. Once she had arrived, the note said, she'd be given full board while collecting the necessary wild life. She was to be back by Friday week with all the animals, so that Noah could start the extra scenes. She packed her bag and set off.

When Gloria arrived at the station she became intensely aware of the bookstall. Suppose she were to pick up another innocent-seeming paperback which turned out to have life-changing properties? She settled for something

with lots of stars on the front which called itself *A Journey*
to New Worlds. She'd never read any science fiction but
she knew that next to romance it was the most popular
genre.

Gloria's carriage was empty, so she was able to study
the notices without attracting attention. All railway passengers have a deep fascination for notices of the most
trivial kind. They find this embarrassing, and will go
to any lengths to disguise their obsession from fellow
passengers with the same obsession. Gloria took in the
exhortation to leave the train clean and tidy and felt
suitably awed by the dire warnings against frivolously
pulling the communication cord. She even took out her
handkerchief and shone up the little plaque which the
seat coverers had left as an indication of their handiwork.
It was a brass plaque and gleamed very nicely when she'd
finished. Then, after a quick inspection under the seats
and in the luggage hammock just in case there was
anything nasty or interesting she should know about,
Gloria settled back to enjoy the journey and her science
fiction thriller.

It wasn't actually a thriller, although it was about space.
Space and the new physics. There is no such thing as
objective experiment, it said, because the observer always
affects whatever he observes. Subject and object are only
arbitrarily split for the purposes of limited investigation.
Gloria didn't want to hear this. As far as she was concerned for the time being, subject and object, herself and
what she did, were very much split. She wanted to keep it
that way, otherwise how was she ever going to make the
most of her second stage? She put the book in her bag
and looked out of the window instead.

Train travel always gave Gloria a sense of power. She
liked to imagine that the world was a stage set laid on for
her to pass through. She watched the fields and winding
river slip past, not caring where she was going, only
enjoying the journey for what it was. She had always

dreamed of buying a Rail Rover and going off to exotic places with a knapsack and penknife. Now that she was starting a new life she might get round to doing it; a sort of celebration.

The rhythm of the train made Gloria sleepy after her tumultuous day and late night, and although she didn't fall quite asleep she realised she couldn't be quite awake either. She was standing at the bottom of a bright mountain. She tried to climb it but kept slipping down again. A crowd had gathered, and told her that she couldn't possibly get up there because the surface was made of glass and she was wearing the wrong shoes. Then she felt a twitching in her stomach which got stronger and stronger. An eagle flew out and, picking her up, carried her to the top of the mountain. Disgruntled, the crowd evaporated and Gloria found herself alone. She heard a little cough and saw the orange demon balancing on a crag.

'What's going on?' she demanded.

'Just a word from your sponsors. Did you grow out of the eagle or did the eagle grow out of you?'

'I don't know,' said Gloria crossly. 'This is a bit much.'

But the demon had gone and the train pulled in at Gloria's station.

After half an hour's walk through red soil and golden palms Gloria, having followed her instructions faithfully, found herself standing outside a huge arch which had the inscription 'Bees Of Paradise' chiselled into the moulding. With a jolt she realised where she was: she'd read about it in *Vague*. This was the famous rest home and health spa that belonged to Bunny Mix.

She walked under the arch and came into a garden where it seemed like afternoon. The air was heavy with the scent of bee-attracting flowers, and there were statues of famous people and famous animals who had saved lives. Then, at the end of the garden, she saw a white house glittering in the sunshine. It was beautiful in an oppressive kind of way. Oppressive because there was too

much of everything – flowers of every kind, tame llamas
skipping up and down the steps, and playful fountains
spouting coloured water.

Gloria sat down on one of the marble steps and waited.
She felt too overwhelmed to ring the bell. There was a
noise like someone pushing a tea trolley and Bunny Mix
appeared at the top of the steps on a pair of *diamanté*
roller skates. The rest of her was swathed in a kind of
weatherproof chiffon and her hair had been scraped into
bunches. She threw out her arms, looking just as she did
in all the publicity photographs.

'Darling, you're Noah's zoo person aren't you? He said
you'd be here. I've got all the cages ready and a list of
instructions and, of course, you won't be working by
yourself. I know all about your mother. Noah speaks very
highly of her. Now, you've caught me on the hop a bit
here, so why don't you go into the dining room and have
some of my delicious honey toast while I finish my
morning exercise. These skates do wonders for the calves.
Soon I'll be with you.'

She glided off and Gloria set out to find the dining
room. A few round tables were spread with cloth and
flowers. It was light and airy and Gloria decided she
might as well fortify herself in peace. A waiter brought
her toast and tea – there seemed to be no choice in the
matter. Gingerly she took a bite. It was actually quite
normal toast, though she knew that it cost a fortune.
Bunny Mix claimed it to be the most famous and effica-
cious cure in the world. She said it rehabilitated your
metabolism. Gloria ate three pieces, and was just starting
to relax when there was a rush of wings about her head
and a large bat-like creation dropped into the seat beside
her.

'Marlene!' gasped Gloria. 'What are you doing here?'

'I've just come to ask you the same thing. I'm here to
recuperate from my little op. You must tell me how the

film's going. Come on, let's go for a walk. I can't stand talking over food.'

She took Gloria by the arm and they set off towards the lime trees.

'I'm here to collect some animals,' Gloria began. 'I've only just arrived and I don't really know what's going on. Bunny Mix is coming to explain as soon as she's finished her morning exercise.' (At that moment they caught sight of the rabbit of romance flashing across the patio on her roller skates.) 'But how are you?'

'Oh I'm very well. I got a letter today offering me a new commission for my ceramic work. I've been asked to design a little oven for people who want to commit suicide with some grace, not with their hair full of last week's boiled-over stew. My oven will not be used for cooking, only for exits. It will be exclusive and fitted in your own home by craftsmen.'

'My friend Doris would be interested in that,' said Gloria. 'She's an organic philosopher and she believes that the true meaning of life is death.'

'That's very impressive,' agreed Marlene. 'But nonsense.'

'Well, what do *you* think is the meaning of life then?' asked Gloria, always eager now to compound her experience. Marlene took a deep breath and twirled a lime flower poetically. 'Truth is beauty and beauty truth, that's all we need to know.'

'Gosh,' said Gloria. 'Did you make that up?'

'Of course,' chirped Marlene. 'I am a very creative person.'

They walked together along the shaded pathways until Marlene saw by the sundial that it was time for her Aromatherapy. 'I'll see you at tea time,' she waved as she darted away. 'Find out your room number and we can have long chats.'

Gloria hurried back to the dining room, hoping she wasn't late. She saw the famous novelist approaching, flanked by two leopards and now transformed to her usual elegant self. She greeted Gloria in her customary fashion, that is she almost suffocated her, and when they had become truly separate entities again, she offered to take her on a guided tour to help her settle in. 'There's so much to see, so much to do, no wonder I am so successful and popular.'

They set off over the lawns. 'This is the famous spa which I'm sure you've read about. As you can see, it bubbles coloured water out of the bowels of the earth. This is an ancient place full of healing properties. We don't use medical science here, we use Nature's wisdom. Nature knows best,' and she bent down and scooped some of the water into her palm. 'The water of Life,' she murmured.

Gloria was respectful and hoped she made the right noises in the face of Bunny's enthusiasm. 'What's that?' she asked, pointing to a huge sandpit with a pair of mounds on either side.

'That,' stated Bunny proudly, 'is my patent cure for the obese. We cover them in a solution of honey and glycerine, then we let these trained ants out of their mounds to chew away the fat. I've never known this cure to fail, though it's not for anyone with a weak heart. I administer my other famous cure, the Vitamin E, immediately after treatment. Vitamin E was well known amongst the ancients as a cure for severe nibbling. I have cupboards full of letters from the once obese. I do market a kit for home use, but I don't take any responsibility for those who fail to read the instructions properly and find themselves eaten away. It's all in the proper use of the ants, you see.'

They continued past the gym and swimming pool, where Gloria caught sight of the pink winch, then Bunny Mix invited her in for a cup of elderflower tea and an explanation.

'We're doing this film, as you know, for the Glory of the Lord, so we do want everything to be as authentic as possible, otherwise we could just use a few cats and dogs and skimp on the rest. But Noah wants the animals to be exotic, so that people will want to come out of curiosity. I've got a list of things you'll be responsible for collecting, though as I have already mentioned you will have plenty of equipment and a few assistants. Time is the key, my dear. We're in a hurry. Noah will be holding the press conference later today and announcing the date of opening, so really, nothing must go wrong. I'm sure you understand.' Gloria nodded and Bunny stood up. 'I've ordered you a couple of artichokes stuffed with wholemeal toast – so good for the bowels – and then you must lie down and rest on this wonderful rafia couch I brought back from one of my reading tours. Exertion after eating affects the nervous system, and we do want to keep you in the pink.' She gave a little trill. 'Like me.'

Left alone, Gloria felt better. It was all reasonably straightforward. She could talk to Marlene and it would give her time to think. Ignoring the novelist's exhortations, she gobbled up her vegetables and went to look for her room. Looking in the register, she saw it was next door to Marlene's.

Gloria bounded up the stairs, found the room and knocked on the door. Marlene flung it open, wearing a bright pink silk dressing gown. She kissed Gloria on both cheeks and hurried her inside. 'Sit down, and tell me what you'll have: Scotch or Bourbon?'

'It is, but I don't see why I should suffer, do you? But if you don't drink in the day, don't worry about it.'

Truth was, Gloria never drank at all and although she was thirsty for new experiences, she had a hunch that drinking with Marlene might leave her speechless. Better wait. And so she declined.

Her hostess poured herself a generous shot into a tooth glass and they sat side by side on the bed. 'I'm dying of curiosity,' said Marlene. 'Did you talk to her? What did she say? What was she wearing?'

Gloria remembered Marlene's nervous compulsion to chatter and so she began very slowly, but left no gaps where Marlene might rush in and start another paragraph.

'She wants me to collect a list of animals and get them back on the film set as soon as possible. Noah has arranged his press conference for today, so there's no going back on his deadline. Oh, and it's for the Glory of the Unpronounceable; but we knew that.'

'Yes,' agreed Marlene, 'but what's on your list? Do you know?'

'Not yet. She's giving it to me later on. I don't start till tomorrow.'

'Well, if she says pigeons, refuse,' declared Marlene very emphatically.

Gloria was mystified. She sometimes fed pigeons, she got annoyed when they deposited on her, but she didn't feel passionate about them.

'Explain,' she demanded in her new, confident way.

'I can't explain as well as James Thurber, but I'll do my best. Pigeons are a totally nothing bird: ugly, squat, full of worms, always falling off roofs and shitting everywhere. No other thing in the world falls so far short of being able to do what it cannot do as a pigeon does. Right, those are facts; so why don't we just wipe them out, shoot them, gas them, have a national hunt week with prizes for the most dead? The point is, in some obscure, irrational, nonsensical way, we love them. There are pigeon protection leagues, pigeon enthusiast clubs, a magazine called the *Pigeon Weekly*. Old ladies who can't afford it buy them food, and eccentric but well-regarded novelists walk round with pairs of scissors in case they find one with thread caught round its feet. This is not commonplace behaviour; this is obsession. Do you know how much we spend each year cleaning pigeon shit off the most crucial of our national monuments? These aimless, awful birds have the power to conjure up the most violent emotions in the human breast. Our pigeon-consciousness is more advanced than our understanding of the oppression of minorities. We care about pigeons. You might not, I do not, but there is a giant existentialist network out there, thinking about and protecting pigeons everywhere from the disasters that should certainly befall them. We're talking about the world's most dangerous birds. Forget your bald eagles and your hoopoes, the fear of being carried off at night by a great Auk. It's the pigeon in the street you should be watching out for.'

Gloria was taken aback. She had never considered pigeons in quite the way Marlene had described, but she was willing to believe it was true, if not literally true. It clearly had a potent hold on her friend. She noticed a bird-cage hanging by the window, containing a pair of lovebirds. Would it be insensitive to mention them after Marlene had been so emotional? Probably, but this was her year of living dangerously.

'We could put these in our collection,' she suggested, walking over to the window.

Marlene roused herself from her pigeon-induced torpor and looked very aggrieved. 'We will not. They belong to me. Besides, they wouldn't be of any use to you.'

'The grey one seems a bit subdued,' said Gloria, rattling the bars.

'That's because it's stone dead,' sighed Marlene. 'It died of shock one night when we were watching an Alfred

Hitchcock movie. I buried it, but the cat dug it up and so I decided it would be best to get it stuffed as company for the yellow one. They get on much better now. Before they were always fighting, and I hate fighting, it's so wearing. I wish I'd thought of it earlier. Still, best not to be a murderer if one can help it, I suppose.'

Gloria thought of her mother and father. They had certainly got on better once her father had sunk into the catatonic state that characterised his declining years. The less he exhibited signs of normal life, the more her mother seemed to enjoy his company. Often they had sat by the fire for a whole evening, her mother knitting and talking about life, her father just propped there, vacant; and at bedtime Mrs Munde would beam and say what a lovely time they had had.

Gloria told this to Marlene, who nodded wisely and commented that what most people love best is to talk to themselves, but since such activity is certifiable, the next best thing is to have a prop. There was a pause for reflection, then Marlene asked if she could help Gloria with her animals. 'With the aforementioned exception, that is.'

Gloria was pleased. 'We'll check with Bunny Mix in the morning, but I'm sure she'll agree. Why not?' And so they passed the rest of the day pleasantly, talking about Art and the Meaning of Life. . . .

While Gloria and Marlene were getting to know each other better, Desi was discovering some very disturbing things. She had gone along to the press conference to help Noah generally slime his way through, but after her third Martini she was bored and felt like a bit of diversion. Rita and Sheila wanted to stay in case they met somebody useful, so Desi decided to explore. She hadn't been to Noah's house for a long time, and she knew he had a fine collection of mechanical paraphernalia because inventions were his hobby. Most of them, from what she could remember, were quaint and cute and fun to play with.

She set off to the library, and amused herself for a while with a fish tank full of motor-powered fan-tails, and a robot with a sledgehammer that cracked nuts. Then she noticed that what she had always assumed to be a bookcase was in fact a door, and it was slightly ajar. She stepped through it and closed it, as well as she could. She knew she shouldn't be there, but the heat and the drink had made her reckless. The passage was dimly lit and damp. Quietly she followed it and, noticing the steep decline, reckoned she must now be in the bowels of the house. Up above she could hear a muffled thundering which, she guessed, was the boiler room. She came to another door, and after listening for a moment, pushed at the handle. She had never seen anything quite like the room inside. There was a huge flat table, rusty in places, with heavy manacles hanging from either side. Above it was a device which resembled a large electric toaster.

'Shit,' she breathed. 'My father-in-law's into "S&M".' Then she noticed a bound manuscript lying on the table, about halfway open. Sitting down on the floor she began to read.

THE MANUSCRIPT

From this day natural philosophy, and particularly chemistry, have been my sole occupation. My attention is attracted by the structure of the human frame, and indeed any animal endued with life. Whence, I asked myself, did the principle of life proceed? To examine the causes of life we must first have recourse to death. I have become acquainted with the science of anatomy, but this is not sufficient. I must also observe the natural decay and corruption of the human body. I am forced to spend days and nights in vaults and charnel houses. . . .

After weeks of incredible fatigue, I have succeeded in discovering the cause of generation and life; nay, more,

I have found it in my own kitchen. Searching for nourishment, I groped in the deepfreeze while outside a terrible thunderstorm split the heavens. Wearily I took out a slab of Black Forest Gâteau and a scoop of ice cream, not noticing in my feeble state that both were in a state of nauseating decomposition. As I picked up my spoon I glanced down at the filthy mess and, realising my error, turned to cast the substances into the bin. At that moment a fork of lightning shattered my window and blasted the plate in my hands. I dropped it and jumped back, thankful for my life. Then, before my eyes, a curious, frightful, intoxicating motion rocked the plate back and forth. I saw new life forms struggle their way to the surface of what had once been vile slime. The bolt of lightning, more powerful than any current I had yet generated, had sparked off vital cells from aimless bacteria. I rushed to where the plate lay, and cradling it in my arms, ran back to my laboratory. As I examined the life forms I imagined how it must have been, millions of years ago, when the same act had created the earth and all her inhabitants. Exhaustion stole away further investigation. My last act before falling into a senseless sleep was to turn off the deepfreeze so that I would have more of those precious bacteria. . . .

I cannot continue; my calculations are incorrect. I have created beings, yes; but they, wretched creatures, are little more than imbeciles. I have taken dead bodies, filled them with bacterial charge: but either they explode, or they become nothing better than songbirds, hooting, grinning and calling after me. I am teaching them to play the spoons because I can think of no better occupation. Worst of all their skin has a sickly white hue, doubtless a sign of their origins. Perhaps I should have used less ice-cream? One of them I have tried to train as my cook, but his poor addled brain can produce nothing more than quantities of semolina. I lie awake at night, listening to their racket, unable to bring myself to destroy them. . . .

I have very little money; all my profits are being eaten up by my obsession. I cannot even afford to repair my boats. When the warm weather comes I will set my creatures to selling ice cream on deck. A cruelty, but my work must go on. . . .

I am coming to hate the sight of a refrigerator. Last night, sleep-walking, I bumped into my deepfreeze and awoke crying for mercy. My eyes rolled wild in my head; I took an axe and tried to cut the vile thing down, but its enamel proved the defeater of me. I will never again eat frozen food. . . .

No one can conceive the variety of emotions that now bear me onwards. I have resolved, contrary to my first intention, to make a being of gigantic stature; that is to say about eight feet high and proportionally large. Such a being will be able to withstand the current. A new species will then bless me as its creator and source; many happy and excellent natures will owe their existence to me. No father could claim the gratitude of his child so completely as I will be able to claim theirs. . . .

It was on a dreary night of November that I beheld the accomplishment of my toils. With an anxiety that almost amounted to agony, I collected the instruments of life one by one, that I might infuse a spark of being into the lifeless thing that lay at my feet. It was already one in the morning, the rain pattered dismally at my panes, and my candle was nearly burnt out when, by the glimmer of the half-extinguished light, I saw the dull yellow eye of the creature open. It breathed hard, and a convulsive motion agitated its limbs. Immediately the thing sat up on the table and asked for semolina.

When I told it I had none it flew into a rage and threatened my very life. I trembled as I watched it stand carefully on those legs I had chosen and begin to comb its hair with hands I had made. I had desired it to live with an ardour that far exceeded moderation; but now that I had finished, the beauty of the dream vanished and horror and disgust filled my heart. Unable to endure the aspect of the being I had created preening itself, I rushed out of the room and threw myself on my bed in my clothes. I slept, but I was disturbed by the wildest dreams: a prisoner within a huge fridge-freezer forced to live on ice cream and Black Forest Gâteau. I tried to flee, but my efforts were foiled by the ever-closing door of the fridge. I started from my sleep with horror, a cold dew covered my forehead, my teeth chattered, and then, holding up the curtain around my bed, I saw the thing itself, dressed all in white, with a long white beard and an ice-cream pallor. I cursed the day I had thought of using vanilla essence as a moisture for the brain. The creature smiled serenely, told me that he was more powerful than I could possibly imagine and was about to leave for a holiday to see the world. I reached out my hand to detain him, but he vanished. . . .

Months have passed. He has taken to living in a cloud. I realised that I must bargain with him, and so we have invented something we call Fundamental Religion. That is, he claims to have made the world and everything on it, and I go along with that as his chosen spokesman. It will make me rich, and perhaps give me a chance to regain control. He still needs me. He's powerful beyond measure but doesn't know which knife to use for *pâté*. As long as he needs me, I have a hold. . . .

Desi put down the manuscript. She couldn't believe it. Noah had made the Unpronounceable by accident out of a piece of gâteau and a giant electric toaster. No wonder he hated frozen food. It began to make sense. But why didn't the Unpronounceable just destroy him? Surely by now he must have learned to negotiate the cutlery? And why were they so keen to make the movie? As she was thinking, she saw a piece of paper wedged on top of the manuscript. She read it. It was a memo, very badly typed, from someone called Lucifer, and it warned Noah that he'd better be at the Gaza Strip to meet the Unpronounce-able right after the press conference. Desi was horrified – and consumed with curiosity. She scrambled up and ran back into the library. The conference was to finish in fifteen minutes. If she left now, she might make it ahead of them and find somewhere to hide.

Mrs Munde was seeking compensation. She had just lost her arm in the Hallelujah Hamburger machine and she didn't like it. It had all happened very suddenly. One minute she was funnelling away singing a little song about love and the lack of it, and the next – whoosh, the thing had scooped her up and made six neat quarterpounders out of her left arm. Mrs Munde was aghast. She had never lost an arm before, and she couldn't be expected to cope with it. On top of the shock, it was beginning to hurt. She rushed up to the big house and met Ham coming out of the press conference. He looked tense.

'How much is an arm worth?' she demanded.

'Mrs Munde, I have no time for philosophy right now,' he said politely, edging past her.

This was not the right response and Mrs Munde started to cry, pointing at the same time to her stump.

'Oh my God,' breathed Ham. 'Did you do that in the machine?'

Mrs Munde nodded and cried all the more. Really, she was fed up of being stoic; what she wanted now was sympathy. Ham glanced at his watch.

'Suppose I give you a new job. Suppose I make you

Editorial Advisor to one of my newspapers? Suppose I give you a lump sum tax free? Well? If you agree, we'll say no more about it.'

Mrs Munde fainted and was carried inside by two orderlies. When she came round it was almost night. Her stump had been bandaged and there was a fat envelope by her bed. She tore it open with her teeth. Inside was a set of instructions about her new job: where she should go, what she would have to do. Then there was a thick wodge of notes and a piece of paper for her to sign saying that the accident had nothing to do with any machines belonging to the House of Trust and Fortitude Group. She couldn't sign it because she had been left-handed, but she was so excited about her new role in life that she decided to forget the little incident and put it down to an act of God.

And so it was that the next day Mrs Munde packed up her little spotty handkerchief and set out for the offices of NAFF (No Artificial or Frozen Food). This newspaper looked after the interests of the great Unpronounceable as far as the daily reading public were concerned. Noah felt it important to have a stronghold in the media.

As Mrs Munde arrived at the offices they were laying out the next day's issue. On the front cover was a picture of a husband and wife standing proudly over their dismantled freezer: 'We did use to row,' said the husband, 'and always at mealtimes, but until we heard about YAHWEH we never realised it was because of the frozen food we were eating.' The wife said that since she had given up her part-time job to concentrate on cooking properly for herself and her husband, she'd felt happier and more fulfilled. ''Course I miss the girls at work, but you have to make sacrifices, don't you?'

Beneath the editorial was a report by NAFF scientist Pierre Puree detailing beyond doubt the discovery that the use of frozen foods led to disruption in the marital home. 'We're all tempted by the odd packet of *petits pois*, but how quickly that becomes ready-meals and oven chips, how quickly that leads to the wife being out somewhere, the children neglected and rebellious, and the husband forced to fend for himself.' NAFF president Lady Olivia Masticater, at the time on holiday in Andorra, had sent back a telegrammed comment on the masterly research of Pierre Puree. She said, 'There is now every reason to believe that frozen food has contributed to the rise of feminism, premarital sex and premature hair loss.'

Page two carried a feature entitled 'The Teenagers Who Are Saying No', a salutary overview on young people who were coming to terms with their cravings for frozen food, particularly the sticky sweet variety. Derek, an articulate sixteen-year-old from a wealthy family, summed up the problem. 'You get depressed at school, or something goes wrong with your girlfriend, or you find out your maths teacher is a homosexual, and you think: I'll just have one little slice to keep me going. Next thing, you've eaten nearly a whole gâteau, and then you open another one and pretty soon you can be on six or seven a day. Then you have to start stealing the money to afford them.'

NAFF promised more clinics and more advice centres for teenagers who wanted to get off frozen food.

Mrs Munde leafed through the rest of the paper. It was very impressive.

'So what do I have to do?' she asked the secretary.

'Well, we'd like you to start with some market research. We've got this questionnaire to help a person discover whether they're really hooked or just a nibbler; and we've got a book for parents whose children want a freezer for a wedding present; and we've just published this, written by our president. It's called *The Freezer Generation: A Study in Tyranny*. I think it's going to be decisive in our campaign. I mean when you know how you've been conned by the adverts you won't be able to give a freezer away, let alone sell one.'

'Well, we all look forward to that day,' said Mrs Munde
fervently. 'So shall I read all this and devise my campaign?'

'If you would,' said the secretary. 'And when you do start on the highways and byways remember to tell us your success rate, so that we can print it in the paper. Good luck. We've never had an editor on street duty before.'

No they hadn't; but then no one had lost their arm in a hamburger machine for the glory of the Lord before. So, really, it was cause and effect.

Desi made it to the Strip and found a convenient crevice. She wasn't sure where the cloud would land but she reckoned it would need a stretch of flat, and accordingly she chose the flattest stretch and waited. She didn't have to wait long. Noah's limousine came careering across the sands, with Japeth, Ham and Shem sitting on the back. 'So they're in on it too, the bastards,' she thought, realising that if she didn't know, Rita and Sheila probably didn't either. Noah was driving and looking for all the world like an enervated cue ball. The car screeched to a halt and the four sat in silence, licking their lips and watching the sky. Suddenly the wind began to blow, piling sand into their faces and sweeping it into Desi's hideout. She was terrified she would start to cough. Then the cloud appeared, brilliant white and seven times brighter than the sun. Desi could not help but be impressed. To think this guy had started out as ice cream. There was a flash; and what Desi guessed to be the great Unpronounceable himself – but dimmed, for mortal purposes – floated out and hovered above the side. He waved for Noah to come forward.

'Hello, mother. How are you?' (At this greeting the angels snickered, knowing how YAHWEH talked about Noah behind his back.)

'I'm very well. Yes, we're all very well. What can I do for you?'

'You know damn well what,' snapped the Lord, reverting to type. 'What's going on with this film? I'd said I'd put my name to the books but we made no arrangement about a film. I haven't got a contract, have I?'

'I wasn't sure where you were staying,' faltered Noah. 'You know how you move around. . . .' 'I will not work with that rabbit woman – what's her name, Bunny Mixomatosis? She makes me sick. I hate that show of hers. I don't know why we watch it.'

('But we like it, we like it,' chorused the neutered angels who couldn't really help being voyeurs.)

'You lot shut up,' shouted the Lord, then turned back to Noah. 'Tell me the plot. Who's in it, and what do I get out of it?'

Noah tried. He was at his best, explaining the subtleties of the rabbit's text, how closely it was based on *Genesis* or *How I Did It*. He told God about the forthcoming booked-up tour to York and Wakefield. Finally he gave way to despair. 'It's for your Glory.'

'And your bank balance. Well, I don't want to be involved.'

Noah realised that the Lord was miffed and sulking.

'Oh, come on YAHWEH. Be a sport. You can't do this to me. I've fixed it all up. I've paid out a lot of money, and – ' he faltered again and this time tears filled his eyes, ' – and I'm your mother.'

There was an emotional moment, then the great Unpronounceable pulled himself together. 'You say you've built this huge boat, this ocean-going ark? And you can fill it with a pair of all the animals we've got and still have room for a few people?'

Glumly Noah nodded his shiny head and God started scribbling things on a piece of paper. 'Well then,' proposed the Almighty, 'Why don't we do it for real? I'm fed up of this world and its whingeing scrounging pop-art people.

Why don't I flood the place and we'll start again. We can change the book, put it out under a new cover, stick a bit on the price. No one will know because they'll all be dead. Oh, all except you lot,' he added hastily. 'I wouldn't drown my own family, would I?'

'But what about my tour company? What about my inventions?' pleaded Noah, beginning to prostrate himself.

'What about my chain of restaurants?' demanded Ham. 'I've put a lot of work into those places, gonna have them all up and down the motorways with little fruit machines and magazine racks and car stickers.'

'No you're not,' thundered the Lord, 'and before you try and interrupt again, just remember my motto: "I AM THAT I AM, YAHWEH THE UNPRONOUNCEABLE."'

'But I thought of that for you,' shouted Noah from the floor of the desert.

'I know you did mother,' conceded the Lord. 'You were wasted as a boat builder. You should have been in advertising right from the start. But that's not my fault is it? I wasn't around to advise you. Now listen, I'm going to start raining this place into a designer lake on Friday. You had better pack up your miserable belongings and prepare to be liquidated. Once we've got rid of the old world we're going to have a lot of work to do, and if you lot don't come up with some ideas to make me coherent to future generations I'll take your ocean-going ark and smash it.'

'This is no way for a son to treat his mother!' yelled Noah petulantly, as he climbed back into the car. 'You'll be hearing from my solicitor.'

But the cloud had already taken off.

Desi didn't move. She was too horrified even to think clearly. Did this mean the world was about to come to an end, just when everyone thought they were making a movie? She had to get back and warn people. Gloria — where was Gloria? Then Desi remembered. Gloria had been sent to Bees of Paradise to collect animals. She had to get a train and see her, and in the meantime, she had to make sure that none of her family found out what she knew.

'Why the shit does YAHWEH want to do this?' she asked, hitting a rock.

'Flood myths,' said the orange demon, hopping down in front of her. 'Flood myths are very potent things; humankind can't resist them. I knew this was going to happen right from the start. Don't you know that men always pee on the fire? That's why they were sent out to hunt in the old days, and much more sensible it was too; but now, have you ever known anyone have the power and not use it?'

At supper that evening Gloria hailed Bunny Mix across a crowded throng of eager guests and proposed that Marlene help her out in the animal search.

'Has she had any training?' asked the famous novelist, overlooking the fact that Gloria herself had had none, apart from being the owner of a pet elephant.

'Oh yes,' enthused Marlene. 'I have such a way with animals. Look at this,' and to Gloria's horror she pulled the stuffed lovebird out of her bag. 'My bird loves me so much he can't bear to stay at home without me. Now, have you ever seen anything like this before?'

Clearly Bunny hadn't, and she backed away as though she might be bitten.

'Oh, don't mind him,' laughed Marlene. 'He won't hurt you, he's a real dream,' and she balanced the unfortunate thing on the edge of her spinach dish.

'Marlene,' chaffed the rabbit of romance, 'you are not allowed to bring pets, however well trained, into this health spa. But I will ignore your indiscretion and yes, you may help Gloria if she feels it's necessary. But remember, this is an indulgence and only because I feel it may

improve your very nervous condition,' and she swept
away.

'Great,' cheered Marlene. 'Now we can have fun.'

After supper Marlene and Gloria went to drink cocoa upstairs and plan their campaign. Bunny had given Gloria the list, and none of the animals seemed too hard to catch, except for a pair of hoopoes that could only, it said, be found in Nineveh in the custody of a rather strange old woman. They were to travel there the next day, on the off chance that she might part with them.

'We ought to bring some order into this,' decided Marlene, and got out the blackboard she usually kept for her dietary progress. 'We'll have to make a list. I'll draw up four columns: Things that Fly; Things that Swim; Things that Run/Crawl/Leap or Totter; and Things that Creep.'

'Yes,' said Gloria, 'that seems very sensible.'

'Gloria,' asked Marlene a few minutes later, 'what did you do before you started collecting animals?'

'Nothing,' said Gloria simply, and she meant it. 'The Cosmic *Rien*.'

'Oh well,' sympathised Marlene. 'At least you've had it easy. As for me – ' and for the next hour she narrated the whole ghastly tale of her life as a synchronised swimmer, a potter and a woman with problems. 'I've had seventy lovers, but I've never found *the one*.'

Did *the one* exist, though? This was what Gloria wanted to know. Wasn't it rather a fantasy of romantic propaganda?

'Well, I expect it is in some ways,' agreed Marlene. 'But in others, there's something to be said for being in love. Lovers take you dancing, they tell you commonplace things that sound different and are different because lovers make you look again at familiar things and find beauty there.'

'Weren't any of your seventy lovers important?' marvelled Gloria.

'Of course they were, at the time. It's just that the time didn't last very long, and the only one who really had any drama was lost from the moment we saw each other.' She dabbed her eyes gently.

'Oh tell me about that one,' begged Gloria in a fit of regressive goo.

Marlene's story was a tragic one. Immediately after her sex change she had fallen in love with a curate, older than her in most ways, riddled with guilt about pleasure that did not involve pain, and unable to enjoy love for its own sake. They had spent nervous afternoons and tension-filled evenings together. On many of their encounters the curate chain-smoked while Marlene sat moodily recounting their relationship to date, and why it was so awful. They had enjoyed simplistic analyses that sounded profound, e.g. 'If it were truly awful we'd stop/you'd leave,' or: 'All I'm certain of is that I love you,' and they wrote letters to each other to be delivered by hand in the middle of the night, especially when it was raining hard. Marlene had become particularly adept at waylaying the curate on his way home from church. They would embrace, stare and sigh, and then the curate had to go home to his family. Once he had gone, Marlene liked to stare up at the bedroom window, while waves of lust and rage convinced her it was the real thing she was feeling.

They did sleep together, once, the day before their relationship ended forever. It was during that graceless and frantic act that Marlene felt the magic wand prodding her in the ribs, and when she woke up, the curate had turned into a toad.

So much for passion. She packed her bags, stared in amazement at the flannel she had used only the night before to wash the curate's bony back, and went home. There she looked in the mirror, and realised she was very far from being the fairest of them all. She was a mess. She had always imagined that pain suited her. It didn't. It made her fat and lunatic, and she realised it for the first time. Her room was untidy and littered with the curate's letters. She put them in a box, opened the windows and started to dust. 'And then,' concluded Marlene, 'I picked up a handful of soil and thought, Tomorrow is another day.'

'Gosh,' sighed Gloria. 'That sounds awful. Why do you still believe in love?'

'Because it's always better to feel something, even if that something is pain. Besides, after that incident I'll never be chasing things I can't have. Now I keep an eye out for the accessible. No more creeps.' She walked over to the window and took a deep breath: 'Come and sniff the honeysuckle; it's magnificent – ' then she paused. 'On second thoughts go and get a bowl of water, because something big and creepy is creeping towards our window right now.'

Gloria rushed across and peered out. Sure enough a dark shape was feeling its way up the clematis towards them.

'It's some kind of Gross Reality, but I don't know which one,' panicked Marlene. Then they heard the thing speak.

'Will you two stop talking amongst yourselves and help me in? It's me, Desi, and I've got enough problems without you pouring water over my head.'

'Heavens!' squeaked Marlene. 'Why can't you use the stairs like everyone else?'

'Because I don't want anyone to know I'm here, that's why not,' panted Desi, heaving herself over the window-sill. 'Individual I may be, but I'm not totally out of my tree. I didn't climb three storeys up a wistearia for exercise and general amusement.' She stood in front of them, dusting herself down.

'Clematis dear, not wistearia. So why are you doing The Lady Loves Milk Tray for our benefit?'

'I've got some terrible news, that's why. So find me a drink and prepare to be shattered.' Marlene found the

Scotch and poured a large measure, while Desi unbuttoned her jacket. As calmly as she could she told her story – the manuscript, the equipment, the meeting in Gaza. 'So you see, the Unpronounceable's an all-powerful ice-cream cone and Noah and the boys are going to float away to a better world.'

They discussed the problem for some time, but Desi was clearly exhausted.

'Why don't you sleep here?' suggested Marlene. 'There's nothing any of us can do tonight. Tomorrow we'll go to Nineveh as planned, otherwise Bunny will tell Noah something's up, and you can go back to the film set and see if you can learn anything about the new plans. We can meet again tomorrow night, here, at about this time.'

Wearily Desi agreed and they made her a bed in the bathtub.

'Don't you think we should be panicking?' asked Gloria anxiously, when Desi was safely asleep.

'Yes, I expect so, but what good will it do? We can do our best to warn people as soon as we can prove it, but what makes you think anyone is going to believe a zoo keeper, a transsexual and a member of the rich middle class? Only if Noah starts getting that boat under way and it starts to rain, do we stand a chance of making them see sense. Would you believe this story? I wouldn't. A flood; when has there ever been a flood? It's not part of our history.'

Gloria went to her room and sank into a fitful sleep. She dreamed she was floating along on a log and all she had once known was floating by her. She was cold, wet and cross. As she sailed on she noticed an orange demon cooking sausages over a little fire. The demon seemed entirely unconcerned about the flood, which made Gloria even crosser.

'What's going on?' she demanded.

'Flood myths,' answered her bright friend sagely. 'What

seems outrageous to one generation becomes a common-place to the next. You think this can't happen; but later, when it's history, no one will be surprised.'

The morning dawned bright and fair. Desi slipped away before anyone else had stirred, leaving Gloria and Marlene to rush down to breakfast, acting as casually as possible. They had nardly started on their dandelion croissants when Bunny came bounding across and placed herself beside them.

'Now dears, I hope you two won't idle away the day. I want you to go into Nineveh and pick up that pair of hoopoes. It shouldn't take you long, and besides I especially want you to be back tonight for one of my exclusive talks in the main hall. I shall be reading from my forthcoming book of poems to give the occasion some feeling. I'm sure you've read about the book already, because the press are so excited. It's called *If On A Summer's Night, A Bee* . . . and I think it's my most mature work to date, though of course I have lost none of my freshness. Anyway, there'll be that, and there will also be a very important lady who's come all the way from Andorra just to share with us some of her life-changing secrets, so do get back for seven-thirty, won't you?' and off she swept.

'Bossy isn't she?' said Marlene, stashing a few of the croissants in her handbag. 'I'm taking these in case the journey takes a long time. You know how unreliable the railways are.' She noticed Gloria's face. 'Oh, don't worry. I haven't still got the bird in here. I put him back with the other one.'

Gloria sighed, and they set off together for the station, Marlene commenting enthusiastically on the flora and fauna and what a pity they weren't going to be seeing it for much longer. Gloria, who was beginning to get upset about being drowned, asked Marlene how she could be so carefree in the face of her own mortality and the planet's doom.

'The planet will find a way back, and I don't think of myself as indispensable. Truth to tell, if I didn't have this attitude I'd be a gibbering wreck by now. Besides, we've got work to do – we have to make one heroic attempt at foiling that cosmic dessert and the little chocolate button that created him. If I think about how awful it is, I'll just sit down here until I float away.'

'I don't know what I'm going to do about my mother,' said Gloria. If she was going to worry she might as well worry about the lot now, and get it over with. 'I mean, she won't believe a word of it and most likely she'd go off and tell Noah. I think I'll have to kidnap her.'

Marlene was sympathetic but not much help. She had never met Gloria's mother and could not imagine the force of nature that was Mrs Munde. On the train Gloria tried to explain, but the more she said, the more impossible the picture grew: the bedrooms that stayed up by themselves, the obsession with fish, her romantic fiction and her belief that only two sorts of people existed – friends and enemies; her star-gazing and her belief that she was an astronomer without telescope; and finally her calling to the kitchens of the world where, if she could not put the Lord in their hearts, she could sneak him into their stomachs on a slice of pizza.

'I don't know anyone else like that,' admitted Marlene. 'How have you survived all these years?'

And Gloria explained that she had survived by disappearing to the bottom of her private pool with a collection of unsuitable literature and a vivid imagination. 'And now I am scrutinising the world for the first time and hoping to reach a state of continuous prose.'

'What are you talking about?' asked Marlene, not surprisingly. So Gloria had to tell her about Northrop Frye and her own present state of probing curiosity which she had exchanged for her previously inchoate state and

would, if all went well, trade in for an understanding of
the world which was both fluent and fluid. Continuous
Prose.

'I see,' said Marlene. 'So your mother is in a genuincly
poetic state in which she cannot distinguish between
herself and nature, and you were in a fallen quasi-poetic
state in which you had no distinguishing powers, but no
poetic powers either.'

'That's right.' (Gloria was relieved.) 'My mother is a
very affecting woman. You may think she's crazy but you
can't ignore her. Ignoring me was not an effort at all.
There was no alternative.'

'Pigeons aren't poetic,' hissed Marlene, seeing one out
of the window. 'They're the most prosaic birds invented.
That's the only thing about this flood stuff that cheers me
up; those shitty excuses for powered flight will be wiped
off the map. Have you seen anything with less charm?'

'What about those hoopoes we're collecting? They bite.'

'I'm not bothered about being bittten. Animals and
things always bite. What I object to is the psychological
reign of terror imposed on me just because I want to kill
them all. I used to have a catapult and a bag of dried
peas, that got rid of them, but then I got fined. Fined for
threats on a pigeon's life with a pea.'

For the rest of the trip they talked again about Art and
the Meaning of Life and whether or not the Experimental
Novel had any significance in the society that haggled
over which television channel should show *Dallas*.

'I like reading books,' insisted Marlene, 'but I'm more
concerned with how to get rid of the cellulite on my
thighs. I mean, there's plenty of books around but I've
only got this one body.'

'Art shows us how to transcend the purely physical,'
said Gloria loftily.

'Yes, but Art won't get rid of my cellulite, will it?'

'Art will help you put your cellulite in perspective,'

replied Gloria, wondering for a moment who was feeding her her lines.

'I don't want to put it in perspective.' Marlene tried to be patient. 'I want to get rid of it.'

'If you can't get rid of it – and a lot of women can't, you know, no matter how many Swedish bath mitts they buy – Art will help you find other fulfilling ways of being a beautiful person.'

'Rubbish,' snapped Marlene. 'If I don't get rid of it I'll become bitter and twisted and start interfering with small children,' and she loomed over at Gloria, pulling faces and gnashing her teeth.

'Now you're being difficult,' sighed Gloria. 'Why don't we play Hang the Man or I Spy?'

'No, I'd rather play Battleships but we haven't any graph paper, have we?'

They hadn't, and so they were forced to talk about the Space-Time Continuum, and whether or not you should write books which clearly fixed themselves into time or books which flouted the usual notion of time in an effort to clear the mind of arbitrary divisions.

'It's not illogical to ignore time, it's anti-logical; and I expect that's quite useful if you have a pedantic mind.'

'Yes, but would you like to see all the episodes of *Dallas* in the wrong order?'

'I don't think it would make much difference,' said Gloria, who no longer had any interest in the fortunes of Sue Ellen. 'But it seems to me that to restrict your fantasy life is the most oppressive form of masochism. And fiction both belongs to and creates fantasy, so why should it not be as wild as your wildest dreams?'

'Well, I just like things to happen in a line, that's all; and talking of lines, we're at the end of ours. Come on, let's find these hoopoes.' Marlene heaved the cage from the luggage rack and the two of them bundled out onto the platform. 'Got the piece of paper with the details?' Gloria said she had, and they set off into the vast expanses

of Nineveh City which, as the Bible tells us, was a city of
sin. . . .

Mrs Munde was standing in Nineveh centre arranging her orange box. It was a collapsible one that the newspaper had given her, and she very much admired it. She was a woman easily preoccupied by technology, hence her intricate and fatal interest in the Hallelujah Hamburger machine. She had been one of the first women in Ur of the Chaldees to embrace fully the electric toaster, and although Noah had subsequently outlawed such quick-meal gadgets from the true believer's kitchen, Mrs Munde had never quite been able to forgive and forget. She enjoyed and made a success of cooking over open fires with the most primitive equipment – indeed, for most of her married life she had been renowned for her versatility with the naked flame and a skewer – but she had dreams: dreams of working in a huge automated kitchen with electronic egg slicer and pre-programmed French dressing. She always repented after such dreams, worked extra hard cleaning the dirtiest leeks and made unnecessary trips to the cesspit. She had hoped that Ham might help her dreams come true without compromising her position as faithful chefette to the servant of the Unpronounceable. She couldn't change the world with one arm though; at least, not gastronomically. She'd once seen a book about people with one arm. It was called *Famous Disabilities* and it listed everyone who had ever frothed, squinted, fallen over at intervals or had less than their full complement of limbs, and had yet managed to do remarkable things. Remarkable, yes; but none of them had ever invented a dish to melt the heathens' stony hearts, so Mrs Munde was relieved that she had not been put out to grass in that great meadow of neglect but had been given another chance to alter history. The box was a bonus, and as she fitted its last wood-like plastic side she reflected ever-more-gladly on how the Lord understands our little hobby-horses.

She began to sort out her material. She had her large NAFF banner, specially embroidered by veterans of the Good Fight who still wanted to help with active service; she had a collection box and a tract she had prepared herself called 'Know your enemy' which displayed pictures of the most common fridge-freezers and their specifications. On the back she'd printed a list of the most tempting frozen foods and their natural alternatives. She was ready to go. Now all she needed was an audience.

Marlene and Gloria were walking down the street, arguing again, this time about body hair.

'Listen!' shouted Marlene, already inflamed. 'Don't give me all this natural rubbish. If you had warts growing out of the side of your ears, would you leave them there or would you get them seen to?'

Gloria said that the type of warts Marlene was describing would be person-specific and therefore belonging to medical science. Body hair was gender-specific and therefore to do with image and cosmetics.

'You mean,' said Marlene, 'that however you're born is how you've got to stay – buck teeth, spotty, maybe bald, maybe hunchback, perhaps dribbling. Why bother to wear any clothes at all? Why don't we just grow our hair, those of us who can – Gold help the baldies – and run hooting?'

'I never mentioned hooting,' snapped Gloria. 'I think you're too concerned with the way you look, that's all. I don't care if you've got underarm hair.'

'You don't care about my cellulite either. As far as you're concerned I could be as matted as a furze with thighs like orange peel as long as I read Northrop Frye.'

Gloria sighed. 'I just don't see how you can be happy when all you care about is the way you look and whether you should wax, shave or annihilate your underarms.'

'You seemed to worry about the same things for long enough. What about the hair on your head? What about

your nose? What about your cheekbones?' demanded
Marlene, poking Gloria hard to press home her point. At
least Gloria had the sense to blush, but she was put out.
She thought her past belonged to her. She didn't want
Marlene reminding her of what she'd been. She had
already started to rewrite it in accordance with her future,
which included drowning. She wanted to die with integ-
rity. Still, Marlene was right, Gloria had been unfair; and
she took her friend's arm and smiled.

'I wasn't happy then, I wasn't anything; you have to
remember that. I was no more than the colour of the dye
I put on my hair.'

'Well you were peculiar,' insisted Marlene. 'Some of us
can lead rich emotional lives and shave our armpits, you
know.'

For a while they walked on in silence. 'I don't know
where we are,' grumbled Gloria, still sulking. 'Give me
the *A to Z*.'

While she was looking, Marlene wandered off and
noticed a large crowd who appeared to be laughing and
cheering at something. 'Gloria,' she called, 'come over

here; there's a Punch and Judy show, I think.' Together they circled closer, jostling through the crowd till they reached the front.

'Marlene,' said Gloria in a faint voice, 'I'd like you to meet my mother.'

Mrs Munde was having a grand time. The good Lord had sent her an audience and she was certain she was reaching their doubting hearts. A lot of the crowd had already taken her leaflets and accepted her invitation to a further in-depth, follow-up discussion at the NAFF offices. She offered personally made chocolate mousse and re-pounded tea to anyone who turned up – a device never known to fail.

Suddenly, a fat man with a box of his own, though not so stylish as Mrs Munde's, hauled himself up beside her. He took off his jacket and rolled up his shirt sleeves to reveal bulging forearms and a tattoo that said: 'Some like it cold.' He took no notice of Mrs Munde, but instead addressed himself directly to the crowd who were agog.

'This woman has no right to tell any of you how to spend your money or your time. What's wrong with diced carrots? What's so corrupting about mixed veg? We've all enjoyed Rum Babas haven't we? And some of us will have enjoyed them with ice cream too. There's not one of you here who hasn't got a packet of *petits pois* hidden away at home. What do you do when that unexpected guest arrives? Where do you turn when your relatives want to come for Sunday lunch and don't tell you till after closing time on Saturday night? How do you cope when your children's friends get locked out? You turn to the freezer, that's what. Side of beef, Yorkshire pud, last year's raspberries; it's all there. Then there's the problem of midnight feasts – you can't have cheesecake when you've got a craving if there's none to thaw out. What about Friday night, eh? Work over, Martini time coming up: where do you keep the frosted glass, the welcome ice cubes? Where do you put the cocktail cherries? I don't have to spell it out do I?

'Forget about NAFF, join SCOFF, the Society for the Celebration of Frozen Food. Subscriptions are low, you get a regular bulletin, regular news on offers to improve the quality of your freezing stock and an annual outing to Andorra, done at half price for all our members. We go to Andorra because as you will have read in the local newspapers – ' (he glared across at Mrs Munde) ' – the President of Andorra, Gary Cooper, who used to be in all our favourite films, has been scientifically and fully cured of his deafness by adhering to a diet made up entirely of frozen food. We have testimonials from him, and if you can't trust a president, who can you trust?'

'You can trust the Lord!' yelled Mrs Munde, showering her tracts onto the baffled crowd.

'I want to ask a question,' piped a voice from the floor. 'I want to know where you draw the line. Can I keep my milk in a cool box in summer or not? It doesn't have any ice and it doesn't freeze anything, but it does keep things cool.'

'If it doesn't freeze anything then it's not a freezer, so I wouldn't worry about that,' declared Gloria's mother grandly.

'This is nonsense,' yelled someone else. 'You want to put the clock back. Where would feminism be today without the deepfreeze? Where would the Salvation Army be?'

'Liars and hypocrites, the lot!' shouted Mrs Munde. 'Give up your fridges and join me in the garden. Go back to the humble larder, the innocent marble slab, teach your children the value of fresh food.'

'My,' said Marlene admiringly, 'she does have a way with words, doesn't she? Are you going to introduce us properly?'

The crowd had begun to disperse, and Mrs Munde, who had timing even if she didn't have anything else, stepped down from her box. Gloria noticed that her arm was missing. 'She used to have two arms, I'm sure of it,' hissed Gloria. 'Come on, we'll do our best. . . . Hello mother, it's me.' Gloria waited patiently.

'Who – who are you?' asked Mrs Munde, standing up.

'I'm your daughter – you know – Gloria.'

'Oh I'm sorry, dear,' apologised her mother. 'I didn't recognise you without my arm. It changes your perspective on life, only having one.'

'What happened to the other one?' Gloria hoped it wasn't in bad taste to ask.

'I lost it like you said I would, in that hamburger machine. But don't fret, I've got this job now, and really it makes a nice change to get away from those pans for a bit. I'm staying in a hotel, too. Do you want to come and look at it? It's got a lovely view of the sky at night.'

'No we can't. We've just come to collect a couple of hoopoes and then we have to get back to the farm. This is Marlene, who helps.'

Mrs Munde said she was very pleased that Gloria had found such a nice friend, but that she had to go and work out her campaign for tomorrow as well as report back to the NAFF offices, warning them about the SCOFF offensive. She finished folding her orange box and waved goodbye, pausing only to warn Gloria that hoopoes bite.

'Well, there you are,' Gloria shook her head at the retreating figure. 'Are you surprised I lived in a diving bell for eighteen years?'

'I'm surprised you lived at all. Come on, let's get these birds.'

They passed on towards the address Bunny Mix had written down. It was an old house, battered and crumbling, the garden covered in bindweed.

'I'm not keen on this,' declared Marlene. 'What a state the house is in. You can get grants nowadays to do up your home. She must be socialist. Who's going to ask

her? I think it should be you. Since you're struggling
towards continuous prose it'll give you some practice.'

Gloria knocked boldly at the door, which swung open immediately to reveal a wizened face that said, 'Go away.'

'We've come for your hoopoes,' said Gloria, in what she hoped was a voice of authority.

'Well, you can't have them. They're mine, both of them, and I've paid the licence.'

'We're collecting for – ' began Marlene, trying to be helpful.

'I never give to charity.'

Gloria tried the psychological approach. 'Why are you so attached to these hoopoes?'

'They were a wedding present – the only thing I got that wasn't out of the John Lewis catalogue. You can have my ironing board if you like. The cover's a bit worn but it'll do for charity, won't it?'

'We aren't collecting for charity,' Gloria tried to explain. 'We're collecting animals for a film. Your name will be on the credits.'

'Oh, you work with David Attenborough, do you? I used to like his films; always were full of animals. Course, that was when I could see.'

'We'll offer you proper money. Here's the amount I had in mind,' and as Gloria fumbled with her bit of paper, the old woman snatched if off her and studied it with the intensity of a palm reader.

'I thought you couldn't see,' accused Marlene.

'I can't see moving things, but I can see still things, long as they stay still,' the creature shot back, and Marlene subsided. 'All right, you can take them, but they're not what I'd call the easiest of birds. You'd be better off with pigeons.'

While Marlene blanched, the birds were fetched, looking very moody in their cage with a green baize floor.

'I've lost the instructions, but I expect you'll get the hang of them. The tall one likes sausage.' And with that the woman slammed the door, leaving them alone with their prize.

'I wonder what the small one likes?' Marlene asked tentatively. 'We could pick up some sausage on the way to the station, but she didn't say what sort. Do you think she meant regular breakfast sausage, or garlic sausage, or maybe she meant chipolatas?'

At the mention of chipolatas the tall bird began to dance up and down on his perch. So that's what they got for him, and he ate it all and the small one sulked, but they didn't have time to experiment because the train was leaving Nineveh and Bunny Mix had ordered they be on it. They found an empty carriage and placed the birds on the seat opposite them, while the birds stared out of the window trying to pretend that they often travelled by train and weren't insecure. 'See what I mean?' pointed Marlene. 'These birds, unlike some birds I could mention, have got style.'

For Desi the day had been less satisfactory, although she didn't have to suffer the shock of seeing her mother converting the multitudes. Desi's mother had been a suspicious woman, given to bouts of bridge and fits of pique. She liked to think of herself as a princess in an ivory tower and didn't enjoy it when her husband refused to participate in the fantasy. Eventually, she took to living upstairs in two rooms and consulting her almanac. She was an expert on tides, although the family lived two hundred miles inland. 'I need something to do,' she said, when questioned. 'I have so little to live for.'

As a result her husband moved out, taking Desi with him; and together they toured the world, collecting unusual stones for the rock garden in their new home. Occasionally Desi sent a postcard to her mother which was always returned saying, 'Not at this address' in her mother's handwriting.

Thus Desi was well equipped to marry into one of the
more eccentric families in the Middle East, when she met
Shem and his family at an auction of semi-precious stones.
She didn't mind Noah's outbursts or her own husband's
obsession with Petanque; but she did think it a bit
much when she discovered they were about to aid the
Unpronounceable in flooding the world. Her mother
would probably have a seizure when she saw the waters
rising without reference to her tide timetables, while her
father's rock garden – his life's work and very pretty too
– would be totally washed away. It was a bad business,
all this interfering with other people's lives.

When she got back from Bees of Paradise she was just
in time for breakfast, and took her place with the rest of
the family who appeared to be in a nonchalantly bantering
mood. Noah was bending his shiny bald head over a
shiny bald egg and talking about his reasons for shooting
the early part of the film in black and white. 'I want to
use colour as a medium for expression,' he explained
earnestly, as if no one had ever said it before. 'I want to
give God the best, the blue bits and the red bits and the
sea-green bits. I want him to have it all.'

'Hallelujah, Dad,' shouted Ham enthusiastically. 'Does
anyone want this piece of toast?'

Rita and Sheila were being excused the film set for a
day to get their hair done. Rita said she looked like a rag.

'What about you, Desi?' asked Shem, smiling as he
always did.

'I thought I'd stay with you boys. So much to see, so
much to do. . . .'

There was a moment's pause while the men exchanged
glances, then Ham wiped his fingers and coughed. 'I don't
think you'd find it very much fun today. We've got a
meeting with our technical people and then a meeting
with the sound crew and it's all work and no play. Besides,
Dad's in a bad mood, aren't you, Dad?'

'Yes,' agreed Noah. 'I'm in a terrible mood. Heads will roll today.'

'See? I told you. Why don't you take a horse and go out somewhere?'

'All right,' said Desi, hoping she was being convincing. 'I may stay over at some friends' tonight – no need for me to be here in the morning, is there?'

The boys were clearly relieved and Noah stopped making diagrams with the salt. Within five minutes the table was deserted, leaving Desi to work out how she was going to follow them. She was sure they were going to talk to YAHWEH again, sure they had some kind of plan.

She set off for the stables just in time to see the car rolling off down the drive. Her horse was saddled, and taking the route over the hills that followed the road, she observed their journey until they came to a level plain in the middle of nowhere. Tying her horse, she slithered down through the bushes, feeling like one of the Famous Five but rather too old. Noah and the boys were discussing their plan, and Noah was holding forth.

'So I'll suggest that we rewrite *Genesis* and make it look like God did it all from the very beginning, and we'll put in a lot of stories about how mysterious he is, and how no one knows where he came from.'

'Who's going to believe in him if he stops making personal appearances? Aren't you going to have to keep this up for ever? All these crusades and things get on my nerves. He's such a drama queen, always worrying about how his voice sounds through a cloud. We've been working for years to try and make him more discreet, but if we start the world again we'll have it all over again.' Ham was peevish, probably because he was still upset about his motorway services.

Noah tried to be patient with his son's lack of imagination. 'If we've got a new world we can tell them anything. They won't have any memory, any photo albums, any pressure groups or state-funded anarchy. We can say that

God made the world, the air, the sky, the sea, and that it
became so corrupt he had to flood it and start again.
Who's to say we're lying? The girls'll keep quiet. We can
write what we want in our book, pass it down and call it
the inspired word of God. Once we're dead, that will be
that, sewn up, a cinch. He'll be on his own then, but I
guess he can cope. Look how much progress he's made
with the knives and forks. A mother has to let go some-
time,' and Noah blew his nose very loudly.

'All right, but I want to take the TV with me when we
sail,' said Ham.

Noah looked pained, and wondered if genius always
skips a generation.

'Son, you can take the TV but there won't be anyone
broadcasting. We're starting again – the wheel, the
plough? God, and I paid for your education. I might as
well have let you go comprehensive.'

'What are we going to do about Bunny?' asked Shem
suddenly. 'Are we going to tell her or not?'

Noah sat down, sticking out his stubby legs. He didn't
want to talk about Bunny. 'I'll speak to the Unpronounceable, but I don't think he'll buy it. You know how much
he hates her. He only puts up with her as it is for the sake
of peace and quiet with his angels. Last time he banned
her from the library and threatened to end her TV special
by ending her, they all went on strike; and that meant no
adoration, no semolina, no music. He couldn't take it.'

'Semolina!' spat Ham. 'What sort of food is that for a
God?'

'I know, I know,' sighed Noah. 'We should think up a
better name. What about ambrosia? That's got more
dignity.'

Just then, the sky coloured over and Japeth spotted the
cloud. 'He's landing, everybody, cover your eyes.' In a
dazzle of smoke the cloud dropped down onto the level
plane, and YAHWEH glided out.

'Hellow mother,' he said, ignoring the boys as usual.

'I've had a bad journey and something funny's happening to my left leg. It seems to be generating a smoke column, which in the ordinary way wouldn't be too bad, but this one appears to have a personality.'

Noah turned pale. What if YAHWEH were spontaneously reproducing? He examined the column with his magnifying glass. Yes, he could see a character forming inside, not a full or rounded character but certainly something that might prove difficult. 'It's your emanation,' he said finally. 'It's part of you but it's also separate and it won't go away.'

'Well, what are we going to do? If I'm God to the world I can't reveal a rival. People will call me pagan and it won't be so impressive being in two places at the same time. I'll be ordinary!'

'Calm down,' Noah soothed. 'There's no problem that your mother can't solve. We'll have to incorporate it — it can be part of your general mystery that you are one person really but another as well. We'll call it something grand and puzzling, like . . . like . . .' Noah sweated for a moment. 'That's it, we'll call it the Holy Wisp.'

'The Unpronounceable and the Holy Wisp? What kind of a team is that?' objected Ham.

'Besides,' butted in the Lord, 'I don't want to be the Unpronounceable any more.'

'But YHWH *is* unpronounceable unless you put some fake vowels in there,' Noah pointed out. 'It's not my fault that we have to do this in Hebrew. It's just how it is.'

'Yes,' insisted God, 'but it isn't always going to be Hebrew, is it? It's going to be French and Norwegian and African and lots of others. You told me I was going to be worldwide. Not everyone speaks Hebrew. I have my popular appeal to think of. Why don't we just settle for something translatable like "Almighty"?'

'Yeah, yeah, at 'em Lord. How about "Immortal Invisible God Only Wise"?' Ham jumped up and down faking

boxer punches in the direction of the cloud. Noah looked
cross.

'Well, I suppose if that's what you want we can write it in,' and he took out his notebook and wrote, 'Almighty'.

'That still doesn't solve the problem of this wisp,' continued the Lord, staring distastefully at his left leg where the column was muttering something about wanting to be a comforter.

'What's that he's saying?' asked Noah, straining to catch it.

'Holy's good, but I'm not sure about wisp,' mused Shem. 'We want to keep the feeling of wisp but maybe a little less flighty. Smoke's too prosaic, spook's too spooky. What about spirit?'

'Holy Spirit,' repeated Noah thoughtfully. 'That fits in with the general idea. Why not try it? What do you think?' He turned to the Lord who was trying it out in different tones of voice.

'Well, if he's here to stay, I guess Holy Spirit will do.' He jerked his head round to the gaggle of angels who were listening in. 'Got that? Holy Spirit. Write it down one of you, please.

'Good,' said God. 'That takes care of the future, roughly speaking, so I'd better tell you about my plans for the present. I'm going to start raining the day after tomorrow, so you'd better make sure that ship of yours is full of animals and that you've got enough food to last a while, because by my calculations we're going to need forty days to make sure they're all dead. Then we can start drying out again.'

'What about Bunny Mix?' blurted out Ham, wishing he hadn't.

'What about her?' demanded God, frowning. 'She's not on the cabin list. That's all you need to know. It's you lot and your wives. Seven, I make it.'

'I haven't got a wife any more,' Noah moaned. 'So if I

want to take a consort, I think it should be allowed. I'll make it legal as soon as we hit dry land. Oh I know how you feel, but she's useful and she'll be able to help with the books. Even your autobiography is going to need a bit of romantic interest and I don't want to have to write those bits. Let her come. We won't tell her until the last minute, then we'll just pile her on board, maybe chloroformed, so she doesn't irritate you. And,' put in Noah winningly, 'think of your angels. They don't have much of a life, do they? Making pudding all day and singing hymns. Be generous.'

God scowled and whipped out his bit of paper. 'All right, you can have her. That makes it eight, though seven's my lucky number.'

'How long will the actual flooding take? I mean how long before we float off and the others don't?' (Shem enjoyed detail.)

'About a day,' replied God, consulting his log tables. 'They won't stand a chance, not when I start the hurricanes. That should sort out anyone who's trying to survive on their dining room table. To be on the safe side though, make sure the river craft have plenty of holes in them, won't you? I don't want to have to do all the work. I'll start the rain nice and slow, just to get everybody off the streets while you get onto your boat, then I'll throw it down like there's no tomorrow. Hee hee, and this time there won't be.' God sat back, obviously pleased.

'What do we tell the girls?' wondered Japeth 'They might get upset if they find out.'

'My advice to you is to drug them along with that rabbit creature,' said the Lord. 'Just put something in their tea, and when they wake up it'll be all over and you'll be singing sea shanties and playing poker.'

The boys nodded and looked at each other. 'Well, we'd better start getting those animals aboard, and somebody should wire Bunny to tell her to hurry up that girl, Mrs

Munde's daughter. She's doing the birds and reptiles, I think. Is that right, Dad?'

Noah nodded. If Mrs Munde hadn't lost her arm he might have tried to persuade the Lord to make it nine, or maybe even done without Bunny Mix; but he couldn't be expected to run a charity and he'd been good to her while it lasted, giving her stable employment and her own choice of pans for all these years. He sighed. The old order changes, giving way to the new. He could deal with it. . . . .

Desi in her bush was horrified. She wasn't going to get on that boat and spend the rest of her life living with those lunatics and that self-aggrandising Being. She'd rather take her chance on the dining room table with Marlene and Gloria. She waited till the car slid off in a skid of dust, then scrambled back to her horse. Should she go straight to Rita and Sheila? No, she didn't think that would work and she had more than a suspicion that Rita and Sheila would be out for their own skins, not the collective skin. Much better that she make it to Bees of Paradise and talk it out with the others. If she used the horse she should be there at about the time they made it back from Nineveh. Her mind too full to think clearly, she hit the road, wondering if a horse could tread water for forty days.

In the car, Noah and the boys were arguing about how much they should take in the way of luxury goods and essentials. Food and tools they agreed on, and seeds and animals grain. What they couldn't agree on were the relative merits of gin and bourbon or who should be allowed to choose what kind of soap they needed to start a new world.

'What are the girls going to say if there's no Martini?' fretted Shem.

'And if they won't cooperate we can't get on with the new race,' said Ham.

'I say we take hard stuff,' insisted Japeth. 'Forty days on a fucking boat with a pile of animals. You can wake me up when it's all over.'

'Young people,' fumed Noah, as he swerved the car round and round the hairpin bends that led home. 'You young people have no stamina, no instinct for survival. You just care about clean bed linen and aftershave. It was different in my day, when you came from nowhere and you were going nowhere unless you got your hands dirty. Perhaps I've failed as a father. Perhaps I gave you too much?' and he became so emotional that he was forced to let Japeth take over the driving.

When the men reached home they found Rita and Sheila fresh from the hairdresser's feeling, in their own words, like a million dollars.

'I hate women who use clichés,' grumbled Noah to himself, but he didn't say anything because he was still feeling insecure about his role as a father, and wondering if he'd made a big mistake all those years ago letting a super-powered ice-cream cone loose on the world. He'd made money and he'd had a few laughs, but what did that mean now he was going to be reduced to a tiller of the soil? He had an uncomfortable feeling that someone somewhere was giggling at his expense.

Morosely, he peeled a pear with the inlaid fruit knife his first wife had given him as a wedding present. Suddenly he came over sentimental. Grace? – why did you have to die? Why did you have to leave me alone with three sons and a hole in my best cabin cruiser? Women – why did they always run out on you at the last moment? Just when you needed them most? Just when you'd worked to get the family home up to scratch, proper carpets, nice three-piece suite, boys at a good school . . . and then

Grace had to take up fencing. Said she needed the exercise.
What for? What did women have to take exercise for? It
was a fad. Bunny Mix was just as bad with those roller
skates. Still, he'd make sure they got thrown overboard.
But Grace — and tears came into his eyes — she'd persuaded
him to buy her a nice sword, the right weight, and an
outfit and then one day she'd fallen on top of the blade,
split right down the middle like an over-ripe avocado,
and they'd had to get her spliced together again for the
funeral.

It was after that he'd started to invent things: harmless
things at first like walkie-talkies and learn-to-talk tapes
for parrots. Then it had got more ambitious, more sinister;
but it wasn't his fault, was it? He was a man pushed by
grief and she had grieved him. An idea occurred to Noah
at that moment: when he sat down to re-draft *Genesis*,
he'd make sure everyone knew where the blame lay.
Women; they're all the same. . . .

When Marlene and Gloria tumbled into Marlene's room
with a pair of disgruntled hoopoes and just enough time
to have a wash before supper, they found Desi already
sitting in the bath-tub.

'Have I got news for you two! Want to hear it?'

'Can't darling,' said Marlene, breathless. 'We've got to
show for supper and one of Bunny's little readings,
otherwise she'll be right up here and you'll be in trouble.
Tell us when we get back.'

'Typical,' thought Desi savagely. 'The world's about to
end and they run off to a poetry reading,' and she rubbed
harder with the pumice stone.

Soup had already been served as Gloria and Marlene
slid into their places, carrying the hoopoes who were now
irate as well as disgruntled. Frantically Marlene gestured
to a waiter. 'Get me some party sausages will you? My
bird's just dying of hunger.'

She might just as well have asked for a bucket of vomit. The waiter stared at her coldly, then shouted something in a foreign language to one of the others. Gloria could tell it was rude because he finished each sentence with 'Hah!' and a spitting noise; but they got the sausages, and the tall bird screamed with delight and gobbled them all up while the short bird just sat and looked sad because he hadn't been fed at all that day.

'We have to get something else for this one,' decided Marlene firmly. 'Eh, *garçon, ici*,' she called. Unwillingly the waiter returned. He hated women who tried to speak French when they couldn't. But Marlene demanded the cheeseboard and a selection of *crudités*, and to her relief the small bird made whoops of delight as soon as he saw the celery sticks stuffed with garlic *pâté*. When he had eaten six he fell asleep on the green baize floor. Quickly Marlene threw her shawl over the cage. 'Let's leave them here till after the reading. If they make a sound while she's at it, we won't get out of this health farm, let alone survive a global flood.'

Gloria nodded, and together they went into the hall. Marlene had stolen a few bits of cheese to keep them going. 'Lowers the acidity level in your mouth — useful for when we have to compliment her afterwards.'

The hall was packed with rustling people from exotic places. The dashing rabbit of romance had arranged herself in the centre of the stage, flanked on both sides by towers of flowers in colours she thought matched and contrasted with her clothes. In fact they matched her hair and clashed with her frock, but no one seemed to notice. She was back-lit with a pink gel spot, and music from her album of love songs recorded with the Nineveh Philharmonic Orchestra filled what space there was left in the hall. Most of the guests had programmes.

'I do like an orchestra,' said Gloria, by way of conversation.

'It's an anagram of carthorse,' replied Marlene airily.

Then Bunny stood up and there was rapturous applause.
She was holding her book of poems.

'My friends,' she began, 'I want to welcome you all to another of my special evenings. I have a very distinguished guest for you tonight who's come all the way from Andorra just to be with us, and I know we appreciate that.' (Murmurs of appreciation rippled through the audience and Bunny smiled.) 'Yes we do, I do too. But first, though it wasn't my intention, I have been persuaded to read to you a few of my poems from my forthcoming book which is receiving so much attention in the press. I have called this collection *If On A Summer's Night, A Bee* . . . because it's about flowers and love and moonlight and those things in life we hold most dear. Ladies and gentlemen, may I start with the title poem?'

There was another round of applause and she cleared her throat.

> *If on a summer's night a bee*
> *Should make honey for you*
> *For you and me.*
> *Be glad.*
> *For we, and the bee*
> *Are really one.*
> *Joined together*
> *By blossom.*

As soon as she had finished the audience leapt to its feet as if it were the Hallelujah Chorus, as if the building were on fire, and cried out with one voice: 'More.' They stamped. 'More, more.'

Winningly Bunny Mix blushed and held her hands in the air until the noise had subsided; then she spoke again, her voice rich and full. She agreed to read just two more poems, then they really must buy the book for themselves; but for the moment she would offer her lyric poem, 'Hyacinths', about stumbling on a sweep of hyacinths and enjoying it, and her more serious and stirring 'Ode On A Grecian Parrot', which said how parrots seemed to transcend time by living so long – which was enviable – but how they couldn't kiss each other – which was their shortcoming.

The audience was rampant by the end of these two, and she promised that they could place orders after the evening so that the very first copies would arrive on their very own doorsteps. Generously, because she liked to show that the very great care for the not-very-great, she promised to autograph the first fifty orders that came her way.

'And now,' she crooned, 'our special guest for tonight. Will you please welcome Miss Tawdry Slattern who's going to tell us all about her revolutionary P-Plan diet.'

The woman on Bunny's right stood up and, after a few moments of effusive praise about everything she could see, began her lecture.

'Ladies, what I have discovered will alter your lives once and for all time; gentlemen, you can have the woman of your dreams, because my new discovery will turn your wives into just that. Remember when every belt notched on the last hole? When the smallest skirt was never too tight? Those lost days can become a reality again. You can walk out of here tonight knowing that tomorrow you begin a new life, a life without embarrassment, a life where you will be able to say "Yes" to any invitation – whether it is a beach party or a seductive little dinner for two. From now on your body won't let you down.

'We all long for romance, don't we? We all tremble with those sylphlike heroines who fill the pages of this wonderful lady's books? We've all imagined ourselves swept away, and then how bitterly realised that it's not the same in a pantie girdle. Too many of us lead a size ten fantasy life with a thirty-inch waistline. How can your man carry you through the puddles of life when he can't get his arms around your middle? We have to think what

men want, as well as what we want to eat. We need their strong bodies, they need our shapely selves. It's called exchange, it's called balance, the mysterious Yin and Yang, but most of all – and I don't have to tell you this – it's called love. Love lies waiting there for each one of us if only we make that extra effort.

'I used to be a Marriage Guidance Counsellor before I became a millionaire, and I saw so many couples whose lives had broken down over too many oven chips and late night cookies. I'd turn to the woman and I'd say: "Slim; your future is in your next meal." As time passed I became more and more interested in the nutritional side of our lives. I have always wanted to help women reach their true potential, and one day, by accident and hard work, I found the formula we need.

'In this suitcase, yes *suit*case, not briefcase, I have letters of gratitude from the hundreds of women I have been able to set on the right path. We are what we eat, ladies. There is no better tonic than the body tonic. Of course, like all the really worthwhile things in life, my treatment isn't cheap; but I know that you wouldn't want to be insulted with cut-price gimmicks. No, the P-Plan diet is for the discerning woman everywhere, and like all brilliant ideas it's very simple.

'I discovered it when my son was constipated. I hazarded that if I gave him as much water as he could possibly drink then he'd start to pee, and on the toilet one thing does lead to another. It worked. It made him look brighter, feel better and he did lose an awful lot of weight, which I was glad about because he was quite chubby. My husband thinks he lost too much; but then we did keep him on nothing but water for three weeks and as I said to Derek after the funeral, "We've made an enormous scientific breakthrough and we can always have another baby."

'However, when you start my fabulous P-Plan it's wise to have a friend who will monitor your fluctuations, because after the first few days you can get a bit light-headed and go too far. We women are emotional. The other thing is that it does demand a sacrifice at the start; you're going to be on the toilet a lot, so it's a good idea to have your dinner parties at home rather than risk the queue for the loo in a strange place; and, darlings, with the best will in the world the opera is out. Now I'm going to close here, and you can ask me questions and sign up at that table over there. Thank you all very much.'

Once again the audience went quite wild: indeed, for most it must have been one of the fuller emotional evenings of their lives. A moment later huge mounds of stout women had gathered round the table, signing up for a course of bottled water. Bunny was kissing anyone who passed her lips and saying how enchanted she was.

'Let's leave and get a drink,' urged Marlene – but it was too late. Bunny had seen them and was floating across the room, accepting compliments as she came.

'How nice,' she cooed, holding out her hands. 'I'm glad you got back. But did you get the birds?'

'Yes,' said Gloria. 'Both of them. They're asleep under a table.'

'How very bizarre,' commented Bunny. 'Still, I suppose you know what you're doing. Now I have an important message. Noah wants you to go back with whatever you've got tomorrow. I told him your assistants had been out collecting the minor pieces and that you were doing the really difficult things, and he said to be sure and get a pair of toads and then come straight back. He wants to get on with the ship scene. So could you leave in the morning? I know it's a bind, but you'll have to get the toads now, won't you? In the dark? Well, I'll see you soon, I'm sure,' and she twirled back into the excited throng.

'Well, that proves it, doesn't it? Let's go and see Desi,' said Gloria.

Desi was out of the bath and reading a detective novel. She greeted them with some cynicism. 'Now that your souls are full can you apply your minds to this little problem, perhaps?'

'No,' said Marlene firmly. 'We've got to collect a pair of toads.'

Desi leapt to her feet. 'Toads? Are you mad? First it's poetry and now it's toads. Don't you understand we're in a state of emergency?'

'Desi,' began Gloria, about to be comforting, but Marlene butted in.

'Just what do you think we can do? What evidence have we got? We might as well go and collect toads in our last hours. It's not going to make any difference. *We're* not going to make any difference, but the toads just might, being watery and not eating much, and . . .' her voice trailed off and she started to cry.

'She's right you know,' said the orange demon sympathetically. They turned towards the voice and saw the creature sitting beside Marlene's stuffed bird. 'No one's going to believe you, but the toads are important. *Tell* them what you heard today Desi,' and while Desi explained how Noah and the boys had fixed everything the demon hopped off and made them some hot milk.

'Now listen,' it ordered. 'Unlike the rest of you, I'm not bound by the vagaries of this plot. I can move backwards and forwards and I can tell you that God *will* flood the world, Noah *will* float away and unless you lot do your best to stay alive there won't be anyone left to spread the word about what really happened. It doesn't even matter if you forget what really happened; if you need to, invent something else. The vital thing is to have an alternative so that people will realise that there's no such thing as a true story. I'm depending on you. History and literature down the centuries are depending on you. Are you willing to let that baldie and his mad family rewrite the world without any interruptions? Or can I trust you?'

'Just us?' questioned Gloria timidly. 'Just the three of us?'

'Well,' considered the demon, 'you could ask Doris. She's still upset about having to be an unbelieving crone in what she thinks is Noah's film. I expect she'd throw in her lot with you. Talk to her in the morning. I'll let her know you're coming.'

'And how are we going to survive the hurricanes and the food problem?' Desi wanted to know. 'If we take a boat they'll find out.'

'Pack up a collapsible dinghy each and as much food as you can trail behind in a watertight container. Hide it all in the attic of this hotel. They know me there. You'll be safe. It might work, or it might not, but you can try.'

'If you're so smart how come you can't tell us whether or not we'll survive?' asked Marlene, feeling put out.

The creature smiled up at her. 'If I told you that now, it would ruin the ending, wouldn't it?' and he vanished.

'So what do we do now?' Gloria was beginning to sense helplessness setting in and she wanted to evict it quickly.

'I think we should get the toads,' suggested Marlene. 'Every year twenty tons of toads get squashed, just trying to mate. The least we can do is save a few ounces for posterity,' and so the two of them set off with a flashlight into the garden, leaving Desi to start packing.

In Nineveh, meanwhile, Mrs Munde was experiencing a very different kind of encounter — not demons for her, but suitors. She felt like a schoolgirl again because the secretary of NAFF, Herb Mill, had asked her to marry him. He had been in the crowd while she had spoken to the heathen and fought off the nasty man from SCOFF, and his heart had been full of the kind of wonder and admiration that can only be called love. Being a decisive man he had followed her to her hotel and asked her to be his wife. He couldn't give her any more children, but he could help her set up a new home with an Aga and no fridge. They might even start a little business — a cake shop perhaps — and Mrs Munde had said, yes! yes! to it all. They could use her compensation money to buy a freehold and a big oven. What would they call it? 'Just Desserts', she decided, as a warning to the heedless and a consolation to the believing. Her arm now seemed a small price to pay for the happiness she was finding. A kitchen after all; not so grand, but ample. She had to tell Gloria, and as she gazed up at the stars they seemed especially bright. 'For me,' she thought. 'They're shining for me.'

Rita was beginning to wonder about her husband. He had been unusually silent all through dinner. But about half an hour after they'd finished their coffee and were sitting watching the television he spoke. 'Why don't we go for a walk in the woods?'

'What for?' she said, not wanting to leave the fire or the TV.

'Oh, for old times' sake. Like we used to. Moonlight ... you know.'

'There's no moon tonight, and you hate the woods.'

'Well, I'd like a change then,' said Japeth defensively. 'A man can start wanting other things and I'd like to walk in the woods.'

'I don't want to,' said Rita firmly. 'Anyway, I'm watching the TV.'

'Typical,' sneered Japeth. 'Other people's wives go for walks in the woods. Why is it you never want to do anything? I slave all day just to keep you in hair-dos and you won't even come for a walk in the woods. I'm not asking you to come on holiday or anything, just a short stroll. You don't even need a coat.'

'I don't want to go,' shouted Rita. 'Do I have to spell it out? Do I have to sign-write it like the Unpronounceable? Just let me watch this programme will you? It's about computers.'

'So why can't you learn to be user-friendly?' snapped Japeth. 'OK, just come out into the garden and we'll look at that fern you like so much.'

'I hate ferns like you hate woods. Now will you shut up?'

'All right, all right,' yelled Japeth. 'I didn't want to do it this way, I wanted to do it nice and gentle with chloroform, but it's your fault.' And he picked up a vase and smashed it over Rita's head. When she was cold he scooped her up and carried her into the library where Sheila was already lying peacefully in a large tea chest. 'She'll need an injection, quick,' he panted. 'I had to hit her over the head. She didn't want to come for a walk in the woods.' He stared at his family who just smiled and carried on with their hobbies. God, he hated selfish people. It was all he could do to make Noah tear himself away from his model ark and give the injection.

'What are you doing with that model?' he demanded. 'We've got a full-size one out the back and soon we'll be in it.'

'I'm trying to find out how porous gopher wood becomes after a period in the water,' explained Noah.

'But that ship's not made out of gopher wood. It's made out of fibre-glass,' protested Japeth.

Angrily Noah swung round. 'Are you crazy? How can I

rewrite the start of the world and then say that we sailed away in a fibre-glass yacht with its own tilt-free pool table? What will it look like? I'm experimenting with something primitive because we're supposed to be a primi tive people according to the story. Now why don't you just go and check the bourbon? I'm tired of you and your brothers. You're going to breed a race of morons.'

'And what are you going to breed?' shot back Japeth sarcastically as he swung out of the door. 'A race of bald romantic novelists?'

Noah turned back to his tank and what dignity he felt he had left. If only he could he'd scrap the whole lot of them and run away with Bunny Mix and a crate of gin. Maybe they'd live, maybe not, and he didn't much care. He'd been the best father he could to those boys, and he'd been more than a mother to that chocolate sundae in the sky, and in the end they'd all turned against him. Well he'd show them. First dry land and he'd plant a vineyard and get roaring drunk and stay drunk for the rest of his life.

The rabbit of romance was in a flap. She had just received the message from her old friend Noah concerning the end of the world. He said it was God's Will, though he didn't tell her the whole story about God's will being more or less his own fault. The message advised her to pack up a small suitcase with her favourite belongings and to hurry over to his place as soon as possible. They were already loading the animals and time was short. He warned her to say nothing. If the others found out (and by others she presumed he meant everybody), there'd be street riots and petitions and trouble at the docks. The Lord wouldn't change his mind so they had to do what he ordered and keep quiet.

Bunny Mix sat on her long pink sofa, taken aback by the sudden turn of events. One minute you're publishing a new book of poems and the next you're being offered a place on a cabin cruiser. As the full implications dawned on her she felt cheated. She had worked all her life and could honestly say that she was enjoying the fruits of her labour. Now her labour was going to be turned into a reservoir. Surely the world wasn't so wicked? Naughty yes, and wayward in places; but really, the idea of starting again. . . . She resolved to telephone Noah at once and make him make the Lord see sense.

When she got through, Noah was not helpful. 'I can't talk to you over the phone. Pack up and get here,' and he hung up.

Slowly the rabbit paced her plush carpet. Perhaps, to be on the safe side, she should do as he said and argue later. After all, with her many reading tours behind her she was used to travelling light. And so it was that two hours later Bunny Mix swept out of her health lodge, trailed by three porters bowed down with suitcases and one cabin trunk. She had arranged for her sofa to be delivered, along with a set of her complete works. The specially bound calfskin set she so admired.

The sun was low in the sky when she arrived at Noah's house, and so as not to attract attention she entered by the library patio and had her bags dropped outside on the lawn. Noah was working on something with his back to her, so she rushed over and covered his eyes with her hands.

'Peek-a-boo, guess who?'

'I can't imagine,' growled Noah ungraciously. Since her telephone call he had begun to regret giving her the opportunity of accompanying them while still conscious. Maybe he should arrange another tea chest. He had meant to do that, but his sons were so repulsive to him just now that he had decided a bit of congenial company might help him get through the worst of it. He turned round and pecked her on the cheek.

'Look,' she said gaily, rummaging in her handbag. 'I've

brought you a sugar pig,' and she laid it snout-down on
the table.

'That's very kind,' thanked Noah, mellowing towards
her. 'Have you brought your luggage? I hope there's not
much?'

'No darling, hardly a stitch, and no shoes to speak of. I
left it on the lawn because I didn't know what you'd
want to do with it.'

Noah walked over to the windows and looked out. 'I
can see three suitcases and a cabin trunk,' he said slowly.

'Yes, it's nothing is it? Don't you think I've done well?'

'Bunny, I told you to pack one small bag with your
favourite possessions.'

'Well those are my favourite possessions, but I couldn't
quite squeeze them into one bag. Oh, and my sofa's
coming too – just one sofa, the pink one, because I'll still
have to work you know, and I can't work with no
equipment, can I?'

Noah toyed with the options before him. He could hit
her over the head right now, himself, in the middle of the
library, and throw her baggage into the cesspit, or he
could ask her to be reasonable. He started with the latter,
so that no one could accuse him of being short-tempered.

'Unless you can get all your favourite possessions into
one of those bags, you'll be floating away with the lot of
them. We've got a pair of every animal you can think of
to go in that ship and hardly room for the sauna, which
God knows we're going to need, and you want to fill the
place up with party frocks.'

Bunny started to cry into her pink fox fur. 'Oh, just
like a man. We women need our little comforts, our one
or two belongings.'

Noah was beside himself, and taking the rabbit by the
hair he pulled her into the garden. 'One or two belongings
don't take up four or five bags,' he screamed. 'Now sort
them out, now right here on the lawn where I can keep an
eye on you.'

Soon the grass was awash with day dresses, evening dresses, night dresses, monogrammed bathrobes, skiing jackets and sportswear.

'Just what do you think this is?' demanded Noah. 'A cruise?'

Bunny continued to sob uncontrollably, and finally pulled out her blue *diamanté* roller skates. Noah snatched them from her. 'Those are too heavy. You'll have to leave them behind.'

Bunny gave a little screech and lunged out to grab them back. She caught one of them by the lace. 'They're not heavy. I had them made to my own specifications. Look, you could lift them both with one finger. Why don't I show you?' But with a terrific pull Noah tugged them from her grasp and fell over backwards into the mimosa.

'My favourite flowers,' wailed the rabbit. 'You've ruined my life and you've squashed my favourite flowers,' and she beat her heels up and down on the impeccable turf.

As Noah was resolving to murder her on the spot — preferably with her own roller skate — a messenger arrived and tried to look respectful, even though two luminaries and notables were rolling around on the grass in a state of high emotion, arguing about clothes.

'What do you want?' Noah snapped.

'I've come to deliver a sofa, sir, a pink sofa and a set of calf-bound books, two and a half thousand calf-bound books.' The man waited for a tip, wondering if all the loose change had been lost in the grass.

'Sofa? Books?' repeated Noah, and Bunny dried her eyes and intervened: 'Yes, dear, you know, I told you,' and she turned to the man and asked him to have them delivered to the lawn.

'Oh no you don't.' Noah regained himself. 'You take those things back to wherever they came from and forget about them. We're not running a library service for the emotionally parched. Bunny, you can have ten of them, I don't care which, but that's your lot; and no sofa. And now I'm going to pack for you since you clearly can't do it yourself,' and with the fury of a lunatic squirrel Noah began to cast garments into the suitcase while Bunny pleaded and persuaded and crawled round on her knees trying to slip things in.

'What's the point of one ballet shoe?' she asked bitterly, when Noah had finally shut the case by sitting on it.

'Think of it as a memento,' he offered, feeling better. 'There won't be any ballet for centuries.'

'No ballet?' whimpered Bunny. 'No opera?'

'Nothing,' relished Noah, beginning to enjoy himself. 'No poetry readings, no press cuttings, no first nights, no honey toast, no treated bath mitts, no hothouse flowers in winter, no mint juleps in summer.'

'What will there be left?' she asked in a voice bereft of its richness.

'Oh, disease and hoeing. Yes, lots of hoeing and rheumatism and the same faces for years and wild animals . . . .' He broke off and decided to stash extra bourbon and not tell anyone.

Long after Noah had gone indoors to have a bath, the rabbit of romance was still sitting on the lawn surrounded by her tussle of excess baggage and the glittering wheel from one of her roller skates. Miserably she picked it up and put it in her pocket. It was dark and no one could see her, and she was trying to decide what to do next. Should she bother to survive or not? What does one decide when Life's Happy Rug is whisked away from under one's feet leaving only the Doormat of Despair? At least these were the terms she used to address herself to the question. She had never been keen on language that was only descriptive. She liked to think that her prose had many levels. Of course she told a story, what novel does not? (Except for those very dreary experimental things that were only fit for wrapping up vegetables.) Yes, she told a story but her prose, like lasagne, was layered. There were strange undercurrents and frivolous cheesy bits and serious meaty bits and a spicy sauce, and of course there was pasta, the body of the book, but who would be content with just pasta?

She remembered her very first book, a passionate and inspiring saga about a cripple and his nurse. In the end they had got married. Two thousand of her books ended in marriage; three hundred saw the male suitor going off to foreign parts with a broken heart; one hundred and fifty showed how a woman rejected may exact horrible vengeance and the other fifty had an untimely death just when the star-crossed lovers were nearing their final happiness. And Noah had said she could only take ten.

She'd bred her very own herd of cattle specially to use as binding for those books. A basic Aberdeen Angus crossed with a Nineveh Nip (so called for their lightness of hoof) had provided resilience and suppleness, the very qualities, she felt, most prevalent in her writing. Now it was all wasted.

She lay on her back, watching the indifferent stars run their circuit, and she smelled the grass, now damp, alongside her nose. She dug her perfectly manicured nails into the soil, her voice breaking with emotion. 'I will survive,' she whispered. 'I will survive.'

The loading of the ark was scheduled for completion that night. Noah had persuaded his crew to work through the night for the sake of speed and secrecy. He claimed he had to have the vessel kitted out for tour by the following morning so that the eager and uncouth press men could come and take their photographs. He promised everyone extra pay. He had never done that before, but then he wasn't going to have to pay up. Noah was especially anxious that the sauna should be working, though Ham wanted to use the space to store a car. He was still convinced that they could start an oil refinery as soon as the earth had dried out. They tossed for it, and Noah

won; so that was a relief. Cars, party frocks – thank God
Rita and Sheila were in their boxes. He couldn't bring
himself even to imagine what they would have wanted to
take along.

They had all briefly wondered where Desi was, but
feeling sure that she would return in time to be knocked
out, Noah got on with the business of putting away the
animals. As they disappeared up the gangplank he counted
and ticked them off his list: two tigers, two lions, two
hippos, two bears, three elephants. He stopped. Three
elephants?

'Why are there three elephants?' he yelled at one of his
men, who shuffled forward rather shamefacedly.

'We got two, like you said, and then we found this one
behind the kitchens. He wanted to come too.'

'What are you talking about?' demanded Noah. 'Elephants don't have feelings.'

At this Trebor dropped a huge tear onto Noah's hand
and the hired man looked hopeful.

'I'll do it in memory of Grace,' thought Noah, softening
a little. She had always liked elephants. It would be a
parting memory before his new life in a new world with
Bunny Mix.

'Take it away – it can come as well,' he said, gruffly,
going back to his list.

When he had sorted out the animals with four or more
legs, he turned to the swimmers and birds. He chose birds
to start with. As he began a little cloud came hovering by
and unzipped itself by Noah's ear. It was Lucifer in a new
hat.

'What do you want?' grumbled Noah, glancing up.

'Like my hat?' asked the angel cheerily. 'We've all got
new hats to celebrate. It's not so bad up there now.'

'You haven't come here just to show me your hat, have
you?'

'Well no. Actually I've got a message from the boss. He
says he'd prefer it if you didn't pack any pigeons.'

134 'No pigeons? Why not? There's nothing wrong with pigeons. I'm taking them,' and Noah started scribbling again.

Lucifer rearranged his hat, which was actually very nice.

'Oh don't. Be a sport. I don't want to have to tell him you're taking them, just when we'd got it all feeling better up there.'

Noah turned round, exasperated. 'Look, this is my ship and my trip. I didn't ask him to flood the bloody place. If that's what he wants to do then he's going to have to put up with pigeons. Can you imagine a world without pigeons?'

Lucifer was getting agitated, so in a rare moment of genorosity Noah decided to help out. 'You tell him I'm not taking any, and I'll take them all the same. Then it's my problem, not yours. How about that?'

The angel cheered up and climbed back into the cloud. 'What a life,' he thought. 'One day I'm going to start my own business.'

Noah continued down his list. He hated interruptions. He always had, even as a child. Grace had never interrupted him. She'd never got in the way, just pottered about the house, smiling and having a gin or two – and then she'd gone and started fencing. He felt the old well of anger boil up, but knew it wasn't the time and got back to the birds. Kookaburras, wagtails, German spider birds, lesser-plumed featherene, hoopoes. No hoopoes. And why not? That girl was supposed to be bringing hoopoes. He called one of the men and sent him to check up. Why, he thought bitterly, couldn't life go smoothly just for a change?

The hoopoes were sitting in a hideout with Marlene, Gloria, Desi and Doris. They'd been hiding out all day, stashing cans of baked beans and slabs of banana bread into waterproof containers. They'd agreed to act normally when the rain began the following afternoon. Desi would go with Gloria to drop off the hoopoes, pick up some clothes and then they'd meet the others at the hotel recommended by the orange demon.

When Noah got tired of the flying things he went inside for a cup of coffee and a hamburger, and found Bunny Mix propped up in his favourite armchair wearing one of his dressing gowns. She had a strange bright look about her, rather like the picture of St Bernadette meeting the Holy Virgin for the first time. Noah couldn't make this comparison, but it did occur to him that she seemed very odd. She was making a list.

'Better now, are you?' he threw out gruffly. After all, he did have to spend the rest of his life with this woman.

'Yes,' she cried, jerking her head towards him. 'I want you to know that I am determined to survive. That's why I'm planning the variations we can do on seven-card whist.'

'Seven-card whist?' Noah poured himself a drink.

'I realise that it would be useless to ask you to lay on a games room, and if we run into storms, backgammon will simply slide away and darts could be fatal. I have decided that a pack of cards is all we need, and accordingly I am plotting the variations on every game I can remember.'

Noah sat opposite her beside the fire. He didn't even ask for his chair back. He was thinking of the days when he had been a young man, poor and optimistic, playing card games on the front steps or down by the boats. That's how he'd got started in boats. He'd won a rower from a lousy card player.

'Poker,' he said smiling. 'You know, Bunny, I won my first boat in a poker game, with a royal flush of spades. Give me that piece of paper and I'll write down the poker variations. Duck in the Pond, Soap in your Eye, Poison Ivy. All depends on which cards are wild.'

Bunny hadn't a clue what he meant, but then she wasn't a poker player. While Noah busied himself she wondered if it was possible to play Donkey with a straight pack. Then when she'd organised the games to her heart's content, there'd be the question of after-supper entertainment with no quartet. They could play charades, but not I Spy because it would have to begin with 'W' after a while and everyone would guess the answer. If Noah would take the cassette player and a supply of batteries they could try Scottish reels or slump in armchairs listening to tapes of 'Saturday Night Theatre'. Her task was large. Four grown men needing diversions, and she the only truly experienced hostess on board.

Noah still had a faraway smile on his face. When he'd first married Grace he'd not been able to offer her much, just a leaky boat and a rented house; and he'd always dreamed of the day when he'd swoop down in a private plane to their backyard as she was hanging out their one or two clothes, and say, 'Climb in honey, I've made it.' After his empire had grown a little, mainly through blackmail, he'd been able to do that, but he still regretted that she hadn't lived long enough to share his real fortune as valet and mother to the Unpronounceable.

'I've got ten ways of playing this game, Bunny. Do you want me to go on to Bridge or would you rather do that yourself?'

Bunny said she'd do it herself, and he went to fix them both a hamburger. On the way to the kitchen he met Ham struggling with a huge TV set.

'Son, why are you rupturing yourself so early on?'

'Dad, I have to take this TV with us. I can't leave it behind. I don't care if I can't switch it on – it's a memory, like other people have photo albums and nodding dogs?'

Noah nodded quietly and patted Ham on the back. 'You go ahead, son. You need it, you have it. Haven't I always said that?'

'Yes Dad, you've been more than a father to me,' and a

huge emotional moment was about to burst with recollec-
tions of the first bicycle and the first full-size cricket bat.
Fortunately, Gross Reality came to the rescue: Ham
dropped the TV on his foot. While he was yelping and
going blue Noah hurried away to find the curried ketchup.
He was running out of reasons for people's behaviour. If
in doubt, he thought, eat; and soon he and Bunny were
tucking into a pair of quarterpounders with extra relish.

'We've got to get the story straight,' he chomped. 'The
story of how all this happened and why. I don't want to
complicate things for future generations by telling them
the whole truth and nothing but the truth. This is an
historic occasion and so we should keep it simple.'

'You're so right,' agreed the rabbit of romance. 'We
explain how evil the world is, though myself I don't think
it merits destruction, but I suppose our God knows best.
Then we say how we eight were saved because we were
the only worthwhile people, and we were saved in your
ocean-going ark.'

'No,' interjected Noah, 'not ocean-going ark. Just ark,
and we say we made it out of gopher wood.'

'But I thought it was fibre-glass with a reinforced hull.'

'It is, it is,' Noah said impatiently, 'but we're creating a
text full of mystery and beauty and we're supposed to be
a simple civilisation. All archetypes are simple civilisations.
How can we say, "And God spake unto Noah and told
him to build an ocean-going ark from fibre-glass with a
reinforced steel hull"? It reads like an enthusiast's magazine, not the inspired word of God. Gopher wood is much
more poetic. Try this,' and Noah cleared his throat:
'"Make yourself an ark of gopher wood; make room in
the ark and cover it inside and out with pitch."'

'But pitch is so smelly,' protested Bunny.

'There isn't any pitch really; I've pine-panelled most of
the inside.'

'What colour is the bathroom?' asked Bunny.

'Pink with marble fittings and a double head shower.'

'Oh good. Now, we say it's made of gopher wood and we all get on with the animals and float away when the rains come, and no one else survives. Then what happens? How do we land? Where do we land?'

'That's the part I've been wondering about,' admitted Noah. 'I've got a generator fitted that should last us a few months so I can monitor the flood rate on computer, but I can't say that can I. . . ? What I think I'll do is find somewhere high up and pretend that's where we dock.'

'Well, why don't we actually dock somewhere high up – we can always walk down again. I'll want to stretch my legs after all that time. I'll get the map and we'll see where there is some.'

Together Noah and Bunny searched through the map until they found Ben Nevis. 'Not tall enough,' said Bunny. They continued their search until they came to Mount Ararat.

'That's tall,' admitted Noah, checking its details in his atlas. 'We could say we stopped there even if we decide not to. I was hoping the marina might clear in time.'

'That still leaves the problem of how we know that the flood waters have subsided,' continued Bunny. 'Now what would a simple people use?'

'A dipstick?' suggested Noah.

'It would have to be very long,' countered Bunny. 'I know; what about a bird? We could say we sent out a bird and that it kept coming back until it found a perch somewhere else. That's very romantic. Readers will enjoy that. We could use a pigeon.'

'Brilliant,' clapped Noah. 'But we'd have to write in another word, even if we did use pigeons,' and he explained to Bunny about God sending Lucifer in a new hat and to tell him not to take any pigeons.

'Well, put down dove then, that's a pretty bird. Yes, we'll send forth a dove, and then when it's all dried out we set up house and live happily ever after.' Bunny sat back, pleased, though it did seem a bit far-fetched even by her elastic standards.

'Yes, I suppose so. At least it will give us a break from the narrative. We can write about what we did later on, later on. But I still feel we need something to round it off, like you do at the end of your stories. There we are beginning a brave new world, walking down the mountain, the only people saved. It needs an extra, a field of poppies maybe, or a galaxy of stars.'

'I suggest,' said the rabbit of romance slowly, 'a rainbow.'

'A rainbow,' repeated Noah. 'Perfect. We go walking off all fresh and hopeful and we look up and see a rainbow. We can pretend we didn't have them before. No one's going to argue, are they?'

He scribbled something on his piece of paper. 'It can be God's friendly gesture, a kind of playful reminder. I can't think of how to phrase it now, but when my hamburger's settled I'll get it out. You don't think it's too way-out for the reading public?'

'If they've swallowed it this far,' declared Bunny, 'they'll love the rainbow. Now that we've got that out of the way, can we decide who'll take which bedroom because I don't want to be too near the animals on account of my asthma, and I'd quite like a portside cabin, if there's one free, if possible near the bathroom. . . .'

'Darling,' thought Noah, falling in love. 'I'll even let you have your sofa back.'

So it was settled, and when the dawn came rosy-fingered through the window they were sitting side by side on the carpet talking about their lives and almost forgetting that today the world would start to end. Such is the power of love. . . .

The hoopoes were chattering in their usual exuberant after-breakfast way as Gloria and Desi carried them up the drive to Noah's house.

'I'm going to miss these things,' said Gloria regretfully. 'They're good company; a bit noisy, but cheerful.'

Desi didn't have time to reply because Shem came rushing out onto the drive waving his arms. He didn't look well. 'Desi, where've you been?'

'Oh, out and about,' said Desi airily. 'I'm staying with friends for a few days, so I'll go and pack a few clothes. Take care of this girl and her birds will you?' and before Shem could stop her she'd rushed inside.

On the bathroom landing she met Bunny Mix in her boudoir slippers carrying a Swedish bath mitt. 'Oh, my dear,' greeted Bunny. 'How lovely to see you. I've come to watch the photographers. You know how much I enjoy the press and the lights. After all, it's my natural habitat.'

'What's she doing here?' Desi wondered to herself as the rabbit swept into the bathroom. 'I thought Noah had decided to chloroform her.'

As she thought this she smelt the unmistakeable afore-mentioned odour, and ducked just in time to stop Shem ramming a soaked handkerchief over her mouth. He fell over and knocked his head against the bannister. No one else was around and the rabbit was singing in the bathtub so Desi hauled him feet first into the airing cupboard and shut the door, being careful to drop the chloroformed hankie in with him. 'Now,' she thought, 'clothes, and get out of here. Rita and Sheila are probably already sound asleep.'

From her bedroom window she could see Gloria and the hoopoes waiting patiently on the lawn. Noah himself appeared, gave Gloria some money, and picked up the cage. He seemed in a good mood, and Bunny was singing in the tub. Maybe there was a new twist in the plot. For a moment she believed that it had been changed, that they weren't going to be drowned after all; then she remembered Shem and the chloroform, grabbed her hold-all and sprinted down the stairs. Noah had disappeared and Gloria was sitting on the front step.

'I'm worrying about my mother; she's going to drown,' said Gloria as Desi appeared.

'So are all our mothers. So are we if we don't get out of here,' and she shooed Gloria ahead of her.

Noah liked the hoopoes too. He decided to keep them as cabin birds – they might even prove lucky mascots. He hadn't had a pet since he was a little boy and that had only been a goat somebody had forgotten about. He'd never had anything exotic, though Bunny had once offered him a gazelle to remind him of her. It struck him that she must have been keen on him for some time. It suddenly added up – the books she had dedicated to him, her gazelle, the flowers she had sent round late at night, and the unsigned card he had received each Valentine's Day. He'd been a blind fool, but then he hadn't known she could be so inventive, so witty. Clearly she was one of those women who thrived on adversity. Not like Grace. Grace had loved life simple; always came out in spots when she got upset. But the time for thoughts of Grace was over. Firmly Noah took down the picture of her which he kept over his safe and put it in the bin. When a man starts a new life he mustn't look back; he must look forward, go forward, he must . . . and he walked straight into his beloved Bunny fresh from the bath. She'd redone her make-up and it would have been an understatement to say she glowed.

He took her hands. 'Will you marry me just as soon as it dries out?' Bunny fell into a dead faint which she later called a swoon, and Noah was forced to drag her to the couch.

As he did so Ham came in, looking puzzled. 'Dad, do you know that Shem's asleep in the airing cupboard?'

'I don't care if he's dead in the airing cupboard,' panted Noah. 'Give me a hand with your new mother.' Together they laid Bunny out as elegantly as a father and son can and propped themselves against the sideboard for a rest.

'Did you say the airing cupboard?' repeated Noah.

'Yes, on his own, fully clothed.'

'I don't understand you boys,' muttered Noah. 'I've given you all perfectly good beds and you still fall asleep anywhere. You were by the pond the other night. I opened the library window and saw you flat out by the pond.'

'I wasn't asleep,' objected Ham defensively. 'I was trying to write a sonnet about the reflection of the moon in the water.'

'What on earth for?' asked Noah, wondering if he should bother.

'Oh well,' blushed Ham, pushing his fists into his pockets. 'I feel stifled. You always want to be the creative one and I'm just a man who sells pastrami. It can make a son seem inadequate. That's why I wanted my chain of motorway service stations. So that I could decorate them all nice, and folks would come in and say what a good eye I had for colour and shapes and then I'd be in the papers too. You're always in the papers.' Noah didn't know what to say, but he promised Ham that in the new world they'd start a newspaper together just as soon as there were enough people to read it who weren't close family.

Noah checked his watch. In a couple of hours the rain would come. Nothing spectacular till evening, but they had to be ready. 'Go and get your brother out of the airing cupboard and load your wives into their cabins. I'll take care of Bunny now.'

Ham nodded and went off, but after an hour he couldn't wake Shem and he couldn't find Desi.

'What if she doesn't get back in time?' he asked nervously, remembering that they had suggested she go away.

'She'll drown,' said Noah simply, 'and that will be a shame, but we can always write her in. Besides, seven is his lucky number, so it might be better for us in the long

run.' And Noah continued to rummage for the magnetic 143
domino set Bunny had persuaded him to take.

Afternoon came, and with it the first splatters of rain.
Noah went out to the boat crew and told them to take
the afternoon off. Soon the grounds were deserted, and
the walkway down to the marina cleared of superfluous
sightseers and autograph-hunters. It was just the family
now, the way it was going to be for a long long time. For
a while no one spoke, and there was only the fire crackling
and the clock ticking and Bunny occasionally clicking her
top teeth the way she did. She was the first to break the
silence.

'Shall we read improving books or does anyone want
to play charades? I don't mind going first.'

'We can't do anything till I've heard from the Lord,'
said Noah, getting up. 'I'm going onto the roof terrace,
and I may not be back for some time.'

'Well, we can start without you, can't we?' fretted
Bunny, but Noah had gone. He came out onto the terrace
and gazed at the leaden sky and the patches of cloud. Out
beyond the grounds the hills were getting fuzzy and the
river flowed greyer than usual. He leaned on the rail and
sighed.

'Was it for this the clay grew tall?' he pondered and
imagined how the house would look under water. He
wondered if there would be anything left after the waters
had abated. In a way it would be better if not. He had a
notion that pain is mostly to do with memory, and the
less there was to remind him, the easier it would be. The
boys would settle in all right, and Bunny seemed fine after
her first tantrum. It was himself he worried about. A
buzzing caught his ear and he saw Lucifer heading for the
terrace.

'Hello,' called the angel, getting out of the cloud. 'I've

come to tell you that we're ready and the Great One sends his love.'

'Is that all?' complained Noah. 'Doesn't he want to know about my rewrite of *Genesis*?'

'He says that can wait. He's too busy getting the rainfall right.'

'Oh well, if that's how he wants to do it . . . but I must say it's a bit offhand,' sniffed Noah, feeling badly let down. At that moment a huge shadow covered the terrace, and they both looked up. It was the Cosmic Cloud.

'Have a good trip, mother,' said a voice that was rich and full, then the cloud vanished in a sweep of rain.

'There you are,' said Lucifer. 'He's not so bad, just moody. I'll see you later,' and the archangel shot off to do the Lord's work.

Noah couldn't help being tearful. He was torn between resentment and pride, as mothers so often are. He decided to go indoors and have a nice cup of tea.

For Noah the rest of the day swung between manic depression and hyperactive jollity, ending in Ham and Shem foxtrotting round the sitting room. They were due to get on the boat at midnight, resigned to Desi's disappearance and Shem's total loss of memory. The rain tapped relentlessly against the windows and the hoopoes hopped up and down nervously. They didn't like nervous people, and Bunny kept trying to make them eat bird-seed because she said it was unrealistic to expect them to find sausages and stuffed celery in the new world. They sulked on their green baize and plotted to bite her finger off the next time she came near. Noah was more sympathetic and sneaked them titbits.

As midnight struck they filed out one by one, and Noah turned out all the lights. Ham was pushing a one-armed bandit on castors because he said he didn't want to waste

all his loose change. The ark lay waiting; and when everyone was safely inside, Noah shut the door.

How do you say goodbye with some grace? Gloria didn't know. She had always believed her world would go on being there. Getting up in the morning made her happy; she greeted life like an old friend and if, like an old friend, she sometimes hated it and wanted to kick it, that was only an excess, not a lack, of feeling. And now it was all going to be taken away and she didn't have a say in the matter. It would be like drinking hemlock, she thought, watching the world drown, watching it go numb and disappear bit by bit.

She stood on her favourite hill and looked down across the landscape. It was quiet and fertile, with the river moving in a snake-tail down the valley. She had seen it snow once, and got up early to catch the fields while they were still covered and perfect. At dawn she had waited until the sun came up, first in bars that slatted the snow and afterwards in a huge expanse of lit-up white. Then, while she watched, a fox ran out, brush high, scenting the wind and pitting the field with trailing paws. She was glad he had got there first, even before the birds.

She wondered about her memory. Would it be less painful if she could remember nothing? Was most pain a product of memory? She set herself, then, to think forward, to think of ways to survive. It must be possible. She and the others needn't give up. They could find something between them. Doris, who always talked about death, wasn't looking forward to it, and Marlene was positively furious. Given the will no flood myth would destroy them. Gloria loved the world; and many waters cannot quench love, neither can floods drown it. She walked back to the hotel and went in to breakfast to meet the rest who were sitting at a circular table with a mound of croissants in

the middle. She slid into her place and started to spread
marmalade.

'How can you think of eating at a time like this?' demanded Doris.

'I'm not going to get many more chances to eat croissants, am I? Even if we survive to build a new world it's going to be ages before we can invent them again. That's one of the things about this whole business that really makes me cross. I don't want to spend the rest of my adult life hoeing turnips with poxy tools and having no books to read.'

'It's better than being dead, though, isn't it?' asked Marlene.

'I don't know if it is or not,' interrupted Desi. 'All we'll have to think about is how the world used to be and how it isn't any more. I think that will drive me crazy.'

'You don't know what's going to be left,' insisted Marlene. 'We might find all kinds of things left over, a bit damp probably, but they'll dry. We have to make some effort, not just sit here being gloomy.'

'I feel like I'm at the Last Supper,' moaned Doris.

The orange demon slid out from underneath the croissant plate, glowing very bright. He nipped Doris' arm.

'Just let's get this straight. I'm the one who can time travel and jump ahead of the plot, not you. You can't be at the last supper because we're nowhere near there chronologically. You've got thousands of years to go before you can get into that plot. We've got the Flight from Israel, Daniel in the Lions' Den, all the prophets and a lot of trouble in some place called Bethlehem, to say nothing of the Greeks and the Romans and the Battle of Salamis – which reminds me, Persia doesn't exist yet. And there's another reason,' the creature continued as Doris was about to protest. 'You can't be at the Last Supper because it's breakfast time. How can you hope to break into chronological leaps when you don't even recognise what meal you're eating?'

'Look here,' said Doris, really miffed. 'You wouldn't like to have my job. I always end up playing bit parts, so if I want to indulge myself in a bit of time travel at the end of somebody's book I'm going to do it. Besides, it was a good line and no one would have noticed it if you hadn't butted in.'

Across from her table were a couple of tourists who wanted to know if it often rained so hard in these parts.

'No,' said Desi gently. 'It never has before and it probably won't again.'

They looked rather mystified by her answer and very soon left the room.

Doris continued to glare at the orange demon, who matched the marmalade nicely and knew it. 'Have you got your stores ready?' he asked. 'Plenty of beans, I hope.'

'We've done all that,' replied Gloria, 'but we don't feel too optimistic about our chances. There's a gale blowing and it's cold.'

'Do your best,' soothed the demon. 'Now, hadn't you better go up into the attic? People are going to start drowning soon; you don't want to go before you've even tried, do you?'

'What about you?' Doris wanted to know. 'Where are you off to? Somewhere exotic I'll bet; some book about the inner life. You're not going to hang around in a damp attic, are you?'

'No,' agreed the demon. 'I'm not. I've done what I can for you, and now I have to go and do it for someone else. There's an Irish poet – oh, light years away from here – who needs to be jolted out of reveries about fairy islands and mist. That's where I'm going. Goodbye,' and the creature slipped round the marmalade jar and was gone.

'Elementals,' spat Doris. 'I hate elementals. They're always so superior, always think they can save the world just because they have a way with words. I'm glad it's gone.'

For a moment no one spoke, then they all chattered at

once in a flurry of trivial conversation about horses and
dogs.

'We'd better move,' said Desi, standing up. 'My feet are wet.'

The hotel was nine stories high, and by later afternoon the waters had reached the seventh. Doris spent most of her time leaning out of the window with a fishing net and a bill hook, catching anything useful. She'd already hooked a whole smoked salmon, various fruits and a couple of garden spades. 'We might need these for our new world,' she explained, hauling them in through the window. 'I don't want to be down on my hands and knees digging like a dog, especially not with rheumatism.'

Desi was wondering about her mother, whose tower would more or less be waterlogged by now. She imagined her clutching her almanac and log table in a welter of uncertainty. It's one thing to be confused in the world's eyes, but to be confused in your own eyes is where the problem starts. All her equilibrium would be floating away along with her husband's rockery. 'If that occurs to her,' thought Desi, 'she'll die happy.'

'Oh yes,' Doris was continuing to whoever was listening, 'before I became an organic philosopher, in the days when I was married, I used to do a lot of fishing. I found it calmed me down. One year I won a prize for landing the biggest swordfish in Marblehead. We painted its bill and hung it up in the living room. I was very proud, but I think that's what killed Samuel, my second husband. He decided to dress up as a swordfish once, when we'd been invited to a fancy-dress party; thought it would make me laugh. Well it did until I realised he was stone dead inside it. He'd suffocated and he hadn't fallen over because the costume was papier-mâché and so it held him upright. Only when I said we'd best be going home and he didn't move did I notice something was wrong. And when we got him out and had him examined it turned out he must have been dead since just after the Martini and olives. To think I'd been talking to a corpse all that time. Makes you wonder about yourself, doesn't it? I never went fishing much after that, I didn't feel it was respectful; but I buried him with the swordfish bill, even though I would have liked to have kept it.'

'That's a very moving story,' murmured Marlene. . . .

On board ship things were also very moving. The animals were terrified and rioting and Bunny was convinced that a python had hidden itself in her cabin. She had gone to feed the reptiles and found only one python, which made her suspicious. She peeped in and offered live mice and warm sparrows, but the other python didn't show up. Then back in her cabin, as she was doing her hair, she heard what she described to Noah as a 'slithery noise'.

'What the hell is a "slithery" noise?'

'It's the kind of noise that pythons make,' she said tearfully.

'And how would you know? I suppose you've been flooded loads of times in your life, haven't you? I suppose you've travelled on scores of arks full of animals, so you'd easily recognise a python.' Noah was cruel, because love's young dream seemed a bit thin every now and again.

'I've been on safari,' replied Bunny with dignity. 'I have seen the creatures of the world in their natural habitat and I have certainly heard the slither of pythons before now.'

'You wouldn't know a python if it got up and bit you.' (At this Bunny gave a little shriek.) 'You wouldn't know a python from a dressing-gown cord.'

'I don't care what you say, there's only one python in that cage and there's a slithery noise in my room.'

Noah strode over to the snake cage and lifted the lid. True, he could only see one python. 'What have you tempted it with?' he asked, and Bunny told him. 'Well why not try a rabbit? They like rabbits, you know.'

Bunny picked up a can of linseed oil that happened to be lying by her right hand and threw it at Noah's shiny head. It was a direct hit and the father of the multitudes-to-be collapsed in a heap in front of the snake cage, a large egg-like lump forming on his small egg-like head.

'Oh, what have I done?' wailed Bunny; then to herself, 'I don't care,' and she flounced out to ask Ham if he wouldn't mind going into her cabin to inspect a slithery noise.

When Noah came to, he considered the incident and decided to put it down to marital nerves. Besides, having a python apparently missing on their first day was a bit worrying. They'd have to talk about it over supper.

'Did you pack those bits of gopher wood I told you about?' Noah asked Japeth, 'because if you didn't . . .'

'They're here, don't worry; but what do you want bits of old gopher wood for?'

'I'm going to plant them on the top of Mount Ararat when we get off this crazy ship so that future generations can discover them, and then they'll think this thing really happened the way I've told it. I don't want them digging up bits of old fibre-glass and speculating on the validity of the Lord's word. We have to inspire confidence.'

'You're clever, Dad,' admired Japeth. 'You think of everything.'

'It's my job, son. I'm just doing my job.' There was a sudden crash and a lurch and the sound of Bunny scream-ing in the bathroom, and the ark began to float.

Noah rushed to the porthole and looked out. 'We're off,' he cried. 'The show's on the road. This water must be half a mile high. I can't see the house at all now.' It wasn't half a mile high but it was deep, and up in the heavens the Great One was celebrating.

'No more hymns tonight, you lot,' he said benignly to

the angels. 'Go and play football or something. This is a holiday.'

'I think this calls for a drink,' said Noah, smiling. 'Here's to our trip.'

Back in the hotel, the flood had reached the ninth floor and the girls were getting their canoes out, though Doris was still busy adding to their pile of useful things.

'How do you feel about your inner life, Gloria?' asked Marlene.

'I feel I can continue it after the flood,' replied Gloria evenly. 'I can think, I can string sentences together and I hope one day to manage a whole paragraph without losing my theme.'

'Well, I look forward to your moment of continuous prose,' said Marlene in a heartfelt and generous fashion. 'At least you can get on with your projects. My cellulite's going to take over my whole body. I'll be like a piece of discarded orange peel and then I'll get hairy because I've only got enough razors to last a year.'

'Two years,' said Gloria, smiling. 'I packed some too, just to show you that I really do care.'

'You're an angel,' cried Marlene, hugging her. 'In two years I might have reinvented the razor.'

'There's someone out here,' shouted Doris, 'in either a tent or a wedding dress, but I can't tell which.'

The others rushed across to the window and Gloria recognised her mother. 'Hook her in, Doris,' she cried, 'it's my mother,' and Doris swung out with the bill hook and caught Mrs Munde as she swirled past.

'Mother, what are you doing and why are you wearing a wedding dress?'

'I tried to get in touch with you, but I couldn't find you,' shouted Mrs Munde above the sound of the rain. 'A very nice man asked me to marry him and I said yes, what with you being grown up and having a start in films and me only having one arm and not being able to work as a cook. We had the ceremony today, but during the reception the rain poured in and my wedding cake floated away. My husband wasn't going to let that happen, not when we hadn't even had a slice, so he swam after it, and that's the last I saw of him. Oh I just want to die, but I can't because this dress keeps me afloat. Why's it got so wet all of a sudden? It never used to be like this in August.'

'Mother, the Lord's flooding the world because he says we're all wicked.' Gloria opted for the simple explanation. 'Noah's floating off in that ark-thing full of animals and we're doing our best to survive.'

'I don't believe a word of it!' yelled Mrs Munde. 'It's just a freak of nature, that's all.' At that moment a sudden gust of wind tore the part of the dress attached to Doris' bill hook and Mrs Munde was swept away into the darkening tide.

'Good luck, mother,' shouted Gloria as loudly as she could.

'I wonder if she'll survive,' mused Marlene.

'I wouldn't be at all surprised,' said Gloria gloomily. 'I don't think my mother's prepared to be extinct just yet. She still has that look about her.'

'There's a whole crowd of people coming past now,' said Doris excitedly. 'They're wearing badges and hats. Looks like Noah's flooded a conference.'

The serious people floated past, bewildered.

'Look, look!' Gloria pointed though she could hardly believe it. 'It's Northrop Frye.'

'I'm getting there, I'm getting there,' she called as he came within earshot. 'I read your book and it changed my life.' But he was lost to her in the night and she didn't know if he'd heard. 'Northrop Frye,' she murmured to herself. 'If I die now I'll die happy.'

'Look out,' said Doris again. 'Here's your ma's wedding cake. We'll have that,' and swinging skilfully with her net she landed it clean onto the attic floor. 'It won't keep, but we can have some to start with. I'm going to shut the window now, otherwise it'll start pouring in and we'll be out there ourselves soon enough. Who's going to light the stove and make a cup of coffee?'

'I will,' offered Marlene. 'Oh, coffee. What a terrible goodbye this is going to be,' and she sniffed the aroma of beans as she ground them. 'My mother always smelt of coffee beans. I didn't like her but she smelt lovely. You expect mothers to smell of something domestic, don't you? I don't mean lavatory cleaner or brussel sprouts but coffee or fruit or hot ironing.'

'Hot ironing?' chorused the others, unable to fix this image.

'Well, perhaps not,' agreed Marlene. 'I wonder how they're doing on the ship? I hope they've forgotten something crucial.'

Marlene's wish was granted. Noah had forgotten to charge up the generator and the whole boat was plunged into darkness as soon as the light failed. That meant no 'Saturday Night Theatre' because he'd said they wouldn't need batteries. Bunny was the only one who didn't care. She'd brought candles and she thought they were more romantic anyway. She snuggled up to Noah and asked him if he'd like her to recite one of her novels. She knew all two thousand five hundred of them off by heart.

'Suppose I start with the first one and we just work through? I can do one each evening after supper.'

'That'll be nice,' said Noah faintly.

'Yes it will, won't it?' cooed Bunny. 'There's nothing like a good book.'

Noah thought of the rest of his life, and his sons, and he comforted himself with the taste of that vineyard he was going to plant. Then he remembered the python and a faint gleam of hope irradiated his gloomy bosom.

'Perhaps she had heard a slithery noise under her pillow
after all. . . .'

The waters increased and bore up the ark, and the girls
in the attic reckoned they'd better be getting into their
waterproofs.

'Last cup of coffee?' suggested Marlene.

As they sat around the stove they couldn't help wondering if they'd see each other again. 'Have we all got our
lifebelts?' said Gloria.

They checked and they had. Doris held up her cup.
'Here's to the future – a world of fridge-freezers and
poetry.'

'And Northrop Frye,' put in Gloria.

'And anti-cellulite cream and disposable razors,' cheered
Marlene.

'And the day we rediscover champagne,' said Desi.
They clinked their cups together and smiled. Many waters
cannot quench love, neither can floods drown it. . . .

'Let's cut the cake,' Gloria picked up a knife, 'and
celebrate.'

A word from our sponsors:

And God said unto Noah, The end of all flesh is come before me; for the earth is filled with violence through them; and, behold, I will destroy them with the earth.

Make thee an ark of gopher wood; rooms shalt thou make in the ark, and shalt pitch it within and without with pitch.

Gardener was very excited. He was to accompany Soames to Ararat to look for the remains of Noah's ark. Soames felt sure it was there and had got all the right sponsorship from all the right foundations. As they set off Gardener asked Soames if he believed in the Bible.

'I think I do, my boy, I think I do,' and then he didn't say anything else for the whole of the journey except to ask Gardener to pass the salt. When they arrived the sun beat down, and the trek to the top of the mountain was made worse by a sick donkey and sly guides. . . .

And the rain was upon the earth forty days and forty nights.

In the selfsame day entered Noah, and Shem, and Ham, and Japheth, the sons of Noah, and Noah's wife, and the three wives of his sons with them, into the ark;

They, and every beast after his kind, and all the cattle after their kind, and every creeping thing that creepeth

'If it did happen,' began Gardener by way of conversation, 'it must have been awful, all those smelly animals and all that pitch.'

And all flesh died that moved upon the earth. . . .
   All in whose nostrils was the breath of life, of all that was in the dry land, died.

'Do you think it really would have killed everyone?' persisted Gardener. 'If it happened at all, I mean?' Soames didn't answer and the patient Gardener finally lost his temper. 'Look here, I know I'm just a junior and jolly grateful to be here, but you haven't spoken to me for three weeks.'

'I'm a man of few words,' replied Soames simply.

Savagely Gardener took out a liquorice stick and chewed on it. He wished he were chewing Soames' hat. He tried to imagine what life must have been like for those people, primitive to start with, but hopelessly impoverished afterwards. He thought of them sitting round their tiny fire perhaps telling one another stories. And he thought of all the ones who must have drowned. There had been a flood around that time, but Gardener didn't think it had much to do with God.

That afternoon they reached the summit and camped for the night. Soames wanted to read and Gardener decided against further conversation. Really, he was a rum chap. You'd expect a bit of encouragement from a famous man. . . .

And it came to pass at the end of forty days, that Noah opened the window of the ark which he had made. . . .

. . . he sent forth a dove from him, to see if the waters were abated from off the face of the ground;

But the dove found no rest for the sole of her foot, and she returned unto him into the ark, for the waters were on the face of the whole earth. . . .

And he stayed yet other seven days; and again he sent forth the dove out of the ark;

And the dove came in to him in the evening; and, lo, in her mouth was an olive leaf pluckt off: so Noah knew that the waters were abated from off the earth.

And he stayed yet other seven days; and sent forth the dove; which returned not again unto him any more.

'Damn good story,' thought Gardener as he drank his coffee. Absolutely plausible once you started to go along with it. He wondered what they'd find in the days that followed.

Soames was the first to find the gopher wood that showed clear signs of ancient wet-rot. It was the first time that Gardener had seen Soames look pleased. He immediately telexed his university, and all the papers jumped up and down and all the Bible scholars said, 'We told you so' and all the born-again believers said, 'Praise the Lord.' Gardener was fed up – he was just a skivvy – and so he decided to go off the next day and dig around by himself. . . .

And God said, This is the token of the covenant which I make between me and you and every living creature that is with you, for perpetual generations:

I do set my bow in the cloud . . . .

'This is odd,' thought Gardener to himself as he extricated it from the earth. 'It looks exactly like the barrel of a one-armed bandit.' (Gardener knew about such things because his father had serviced them at funfairs.) How had it got here? And why was it covered in ante-diluvian slime? He put it to one side and continued. The next thing he found was a message in a bottle. It was written on parchment he guessed, and therefore the bottle would have to be skilfully broken in order to get it out.

He rushed back to Soames who was still packing the gopher wood. Soames examined it, then carelessly broke open the bottle. He deciphered the writing. '"Hey girls, I made it,"' he read slowly, '"love D . . ." D what?' Here he faltered. 'Dorcas?' Gardener craned his neck to read it, then he cleared his throat. 'With respect, sir, it looks like Doris.'

Soames turned on him, his face purple with rage. 'Don't joke with me. You did this, didn't you? Some kind of revenge, eh? I know your type. What kind of a cheap hoax is this?' and he tore up the parchment and threw the bottle over the mountainside. 'Doris! What kind of a name is Doris? If you want to joke, show some flair,' and he stomped into his tent, leaving Gardener nonplussed. It was the longest sentence Soames had spoken, but that didn't help.

The next day Gardener found what looked like an ancient bottle dump – in fact it looked like a French farmer's back yard. Gardener ignored it. It was all a bad dream. . . .

And Noah began to be an husbandman, and he planted a vineyard:
   And he drank of the wine, and was drunken. . . .

The morning after, Gardener asked to be sent home. He didn't say why. In fact he'd found a book, clearly thousands of years old, bound in a tough animal skin unlike anything Gardener had come across before. As he turned the brittle pages – only a few left and most of them badly discoloured – he had the horrible feeling that his mind had gone. He could read Hebrew, he could read Sanscrit, he could read hieroglyphs and had done so accurately many times before. But what he was reading now, while in a recognisable combination of languages, was quite ridiculous. If he hadn't known better he would have said it was part of a romantic novel; and in the bit he had, the heroine was in the kitchen whipping up a mushroom *soufflé*.

He kept the book. He still has it, and friends admire it as a clever joke and roar with laughter when he starts to translate it. 'Gardener,' they say to one another. 'What a sense of humour.'

But for Gardener himself as he grows older and more esteemed the question comes back and back. 'Where did it come from? Who wrote it? And Doris, who was she?' And he answers himself time and time again as he walks down English lanes watching the stars: 'God knows,' he says. 'God knows!'